PIRATES YOU DON'T KNOW,

AND OTHER ADVENTURES IN THE

EXAMINED LIFE

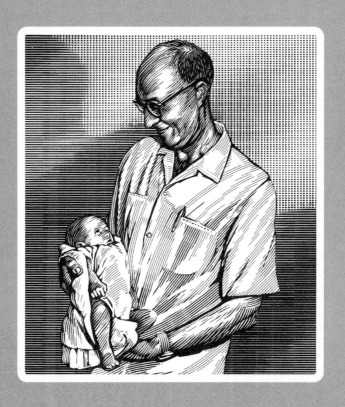

PIRATES
YOU DON'T KNOW,
and Other Adventures *in the*
Examined Life

{ COLLECTED ESSAYS }

John Griswold

The University of Georgia Press
ATHENS & LONDON

Published by the University of Georgia Press

Athens, Georgia 30602

www.ugapress.org

© 2014 by John Griswold

All rights reserved

Designed by Erin Kirk New

Set in Adobe Caslon

Manufactured by Sheridan Books

The paper in this book meets the guidelines for
permanence and durability of the Committee on
Production Guidelines for Book Longevity of the
Council on Library Resources.

Most University of Georgia Press titles are
available from popular e-book vendors.

Printed in the United States of America

14 15 16 17 18 P 5 4 3 2 1

Library of Congress Cataloging-in-Publication Data

Griswold, John.

[Essays. Selections]

Pirates you don't know, and other adventures in the examined life :
collected essays / John Griswold.

pages cm

ISBN-13: 978-0-8203-4678-6 (paperback)

ISBN-10: 0-8203-4678-0 (paperback)

I. Title.

PS3607.R583A6 2014

814'.6—dc23

[B]   2013043431

British Library Cataloging-in-Publication Data available

For James P. Leveille and Charlie S. Jensen,
friends of a lifetime and greater
influences than 10,000
academics.

Better a witty fool than a foolish wit.

—*Twelfth Night*, 1.5.36

Contents

Acknowledgments

Versions of essays in this book first appeared in *Inside Higher Ed; McSweeney's Internet Tendency; Ninth Letter; Brevity;* and *The Best Creative Nonfiction,* Vol. 3. "I Didn't Know" was first published as a poem with line breaks in *War, Literature and the Arts: An International Journal of the Humanities.* A portion of "The Unlikelihood of Fathers" was listed in *Best American Nonrequired Reading, 2009.* My gratitude to the editors of those publications, especially Doug Lederman at *Inside Higher Ed* and John Warner at *McSweeney's,* who supported me so generously, beginning, middle, and end.

Thanks to everyone at the University of Georgia Press, especially Director Lisa Bayer, one good egg.

Thanks also to Katya Cummins, Melanie Hobson, Debra Monroe, and John Warner, again, who suggested pieces, sequence, and focus from the bucket load of stuff I've published under the pen name Oronte Churm, and to Steve Davenport, who made himself interesting first and useful second, as always.

My love and thanks to *all* the nonfiction characters in my life, especially my sons, Jack and Julian, without whom I would be sunk.

PIRATES YOU DON'T KNOW,

AND OTHER ADVENTURES IN THE

EXAMINED LIFE

The Pirate's Waltz

{ 1 }

The box is important, because it's part to the whole, as "sails on the horizon" stand for ships, men, and cannon of the pursuing navy.

The box has ambitions: it wants to mean something *else*. The ridiculous pretensions of a fraught little box.

The box is inconsequential, corrugated and glue, a standard medium container meant to hold only as many books as we can safely carry. It's beginning to fail from fatigue and wear, and the faint tang of cat piss rises as it warms in the sun. I've hauled it around for twenty years as if it were a symbiotic creature, both burden and need, buried in the humid gut of a basement.

Now I've pulled it out into the light for what I hope is the final time, to rid myself of it and signal what follows in these pages.

What follows is not about boxes.
What follows *is* about boxes.
This book is a box, like any other box.
Fuck me to tears.

{ 2 }

A subcategory of tragic characters: beautiful losers. Not pretty people with low ambition or no talent. On the contrary: those who set off full of abilities but are quashed when the soul breaks its shrouds. I've known so many of them, in cities, towns, the military, corporations, and universities that I've begun to wonder if they're America's main product, its most-wasted resource.

Take my mother, please. Privileged last child of an adoring family, the college brat, the beauty. Secret wife, secret divorcée, secret adventurer. Grad student. Teacher. Wife again. Wife *again*. The abused. Virgin mother. The imperially middle-class American lady of the 1960s, fresh back from residence in Asia, taking classes at the university in origami and ikebana. Wit and brilliant mimic. Man-hater. Welfare statistic. Factory worker. Abuser. Crazy cat lady. The crone.

I've reacted cruelly to beautiful losers, out of fear and self-flattery—as if I might have talents on their scale and end as they ended. I blamed my mother for being one. But what parasitic blame do I bear?

{ 3 }

Maybe, in addition to being colorful and bawdy, pirates offer hope that daring will defeat privation and be rewarded with glut. "Who Dares, Wins," as our friends in the Special Air Service say.

Pirates refuse allegiance and romance only the self. The roguish pirate like a rock star, drunk and stranded with the governor's daughter on a deserted isle, would be no gentleman as portrayed.

Real pirates are killed with single bullets by SEAL snipers, whose virtuosity we praise. The rotting corpses of real pirates are hung at the mouth of the Thames as warning: Go your own way and you'll go that way, apart from happy society, for all eternity.

Eve turned to piracy under a perfect reign and headed for the new world, a wormy apple on her ensign. Pandora opened her treasure box to gain some control over a limited life.

{ 1 }

To box—a sporting fight.

To box (someone's ears)—the use of unequal force, as an aristocrat might thrash a beggar in Trollope, or an adult hit a child.

Box (up)—to be done with, to prepare for storage, disposal, forgetting.

Box (in)—to contain or control.

Box—the thing to think outside of. A warning of what we must escape if we're to become our own persons. Once we're out of the box, of course, there's no going back in, though many have tried.

Box—slang for the vagina, because it's what the penis comes in. You can't have my virginity, but you can have the box it was wrapped in. Etc.

Box—container of all the evils of the world, actually a large clay or bronze jar for grain or wine. The persistence in culture that a woman put us all on the wrong path. But even Zeus wasn't mad when Pandora opened it. Why would he be? It's in our nature to want to know, the same frame-up as Eve's. And wasn't the evil released merely complexity, which created even more desire to know? I thought humankind's distinction and chief merit was its questing for understanding.

{ 2 }

My mother decorated with art objects she'd bought abroad. There were also many books, an upright piano, an antique desk from her Daddy, pools of warm light over lamp tables made from Vietnamese fish traps. On top of the encyclopedia, a bronze bust of Teddy Roosevelt, who spoke well of union head John Mitchell and once toured a mine in my hometown. In the closet, boxes of slides from our travels, unused family Bibles, my father's rusting rifle.

We had guests, then—family, family friends, friendly professors who'd been overseas with my folks and sided with my mother. I'd perform as long as possible so I didn't have to say goodnight. She dressed well, company or not. Many nights we read together alone, my cheek resting on her scratchy warm stockinged leg. Everything she did, she did for me, she said.

{ 3 }

Let's say you had a pirate for a mother. To whom are you held hostage? What is proper tribute?

My mother was stern, humorous, attentive, brilliant, quietly wrathful. Intellectually independent and emotionally anarchical, she could be withering about hypocrisy, including that of her culture with its veneer of order and civility over deep sexism, racism, and injustice. But to whom was she a danger?

{ 1 }

They're sexy, good sturdy boxes: crisp and square at the corners, useful for neatly hiding little loved things. We reopen them with the joy of children digging in the toy chest in a family restaurant, where we get to take one thing, if we're good and eat all we're given.

Inside this particular box there'll be a celluloid crib toy, still jangling eerily out of tune. A child's winter coat small enough to fit a teddy bear. Personal letters, divorce decree, a clipping from a Dear Abby column about estranged children, scouting streamers, scraps of paper on which she jotted suspicious license plate numbers and comments that strangers made about her in the aisles in the Walmart.

Each of our hoardings, in its inscrutable method, is its own Cornell Box. At the bottom of hers, a three-ring binder, blue burlap cover, inch-and-a-half spine. Inside the binder, lined sheets with handwritten poems. But what's inside the words?

{ 2 }

What story have *I* been trying to tell, all along? The family tree story, the apple-of-her-eye story, the where-did-everyone-go story, the apple-doesn't-fall-far-from-the-tree story?

I'm probably a teacher because of her, a writer because of her. What else am I probably because of her?

{ 3 }

Pirates and beautiful losers are similar because they both secretly intend to escape before the ceremony is over. Their difference may be merely sturdiness.

A refrigerator box in a closet, bare bulb overhead like cartoon inspiration. I'd stand on a chair and slide into it headfirst like a snake, sit cross-legged on my precious kid junk—cereal-box toys, Big Little Books, leftover pieces from dismantled board games—and consider the exotic coins and army medals I took without permission from the shed out back, which we called The Junkhouse.

{ 1 }

She said things that do not bode well for the poetry: that her Daddy was a senator (state of Illinois, not U.S.), president of the UMWA (district, interim), and a fine man (true, but he also helped trigger an infamous mine war). She introduced herself as an English teacher (elementary school), and my father, she said, was a professor of metallurgy (vocational technology). In Vietnam, she said, we lived in a compound with diplomats (actually all sorts of Americans and other foreigners, including administrators, construction company workers, and military families). She loved certificates, ceremonies, and uniforms.

Some of her ambition, like the destructive heat of background radiation, is in me, her final child and maybe the last American colonial born in the former Indochina. In the box there are photographs of me dressed like a proper little French boy.

The Junkhouse caught things jettisoned from that life after a series of common disasters: my father left us, my mother's mother died and her children squabbled over the estate, and my mother could find no work in her field—or was cheated out of it, which was her take. Among the extra furniture, holiday decorations, boxes of linens, and tools never to be used again was my stroller, four feet long and built like something from a previous century—wood, bamboo, and rattan with wooden discs for wheels held on with wooden cotter pins—in which hissing, yellow-fanged possums raised their own babies.

{ 2 }

I was born fatherless, an act of parthenogenesis, near as I could tell, in Saigon, Vietnam, a city that no longer exists, and was raised by women and the ghosts of men in southern Illinois. There was a lot of romance to that, but it gave wrong ideas. What sometimes looked to me like a fully manned brigantine running downwind, spray curling back from the bow, was really a wreck on a sandbar with a lone survivor.

There were good, even idyllic, years. She bought one of the first Toyotas in the country, a boxy little white station wagon on which she'd raise anchor at first mention in the newspaper of something to see or do. My sister sewed an enormous red pillow for the cargo area, on which I napped, read, and studied the landscape unrestrained. I often brought a friend, and later my mother served as den mother for more boys. We went everywhere in a 300-mile radius and loved that car. But one day she basically gave it away for what she guessed was a "loose wire in the transmission." What it needed was new plugs and to be timed. I blamed her for that, and for not moving to get a job to sustain us, but by then it was too late; the trap had sprung.

Every time the furnace quit when I was a child, I climbed on top of the refrigerator with a blanket because it was warmer near the ceiling, and heat from the coil was trapped under cabinets where my mother kept her most delicate precious things: china, crystal, Vietnamese vases and earthenware mud figures.

An unrepaired leak in the roof led to ceiling collapse in one room and then another; when the smell of damp and mold got too strong we closed door after door. Our one toilet was held by its drain pipe from falling into the crawlspace. The kitchen faucet and tub spigot worked, but not the shower, the stove, the oven, the washer or dryer. Only one or two electrical lights would come on in the house, and there never had been air conditioning. Metal cabinets went furry with rust. Mattresses sagged to the floor.

Her collecting turned: newspapers, cats, dogs, garbage. The animals weren't allowed out of the house for fear they'd run away or be run over on the street, so the floors cupped, warped, and stank from animal waste. I came in once to find the most recent litter of swollen-bellied puppies eating the intestines from the belly of a sick cat, which lay still and looked at me resignedly.

I was often hungry, underweight, dirty, sick, and I had an uncorrected malocclusion of the jaw that made me look like I was frowning. She'd rail for hours about my attitude: Why do you always look so unhappy?

I stole food, but let's not romanticize—I also stole liquor, porn, and other things when stealing turned out to be easy. My mother didn't catch me (after that first time) but told me anyway her mother had said I'd wind up in the poorhouse or jail. Because my father was a complete nonentity, I didn't even understand others' judgments on a boy growing up without one and merely thought: How could my grandmother (she was never Grandma), who died when I was two, know *where* I'd wind up? My mother added that I was a chip off the old block, the son of the devil. Once, after I angered her, she said in a high breathless voice, "You're growing up. If the war in Vietnam goes on much longer, you could have been born and died there too."

Despite all this I did reasonably well in school and was accepted in the engineering program at the University of Illinois, but she refused to let her tax records be used for my financial aid. (The reason why was revealed years later, when she was audited and fined for not reporting some pittance of income from my father.) For half a year I struggled along at a nearby community college. When I gave blood there one day she accused me of doing hard drugs, because she saw my tracks. It was the same reasoning that made it clear the garbage men signified things by the way they stacked emptied cans.

My mother told me, on the day I enlisted in order to get away, that if I got maimed in training I'd better hope they put me in a nursing home, because she sure wasn't going to take care of me. I punished her by accepting her offer to drive me to my first duty station but refusing to sign her in to the PX, which she wanted to see very badly for some World War II notion of what a PX was. Then, estrangement, for nearly twenty years, during which I tried to create a life from scratch and she lived in her hovel.

Sometimes I wondered if she tried to save me by setting me adrift with no provisions, hoping I'd make landfall by sheer luck.

{ 3 }

Not much can live in the surf zone, that tumult between land and sea, except certain species of clams and crabs. Similarly, we crisscross the narrow barren between past and present at our own peril, since the persons we are end *now*. (And now.) (And now.) It's a writer's chief problem.

Memory—a little surprised to find itself still alive after being cast ashore—plants its flag in the sand, holds aloft its holy book of experience and proclaims everything as its own. Meanwhile, the present has already run back out between memory's pointed sabatons to find its own level, since its only and eternal concern is to rejoin the great mass of itself.

Comically, memory never even guesses at the present's depths—the present presents presents we have no capacity to receive—and instead turns its eyes greedily to the country before it. It dons its helmet, raises its halberd, and begins to poke around, sure that there's gold in them hills. Those who arrived in that country first watch jealously from the dunes and sharpen the tips of their quills.

{ 1 }

The box contains the stories we've told since birth, all the stories we'll ever tell.

If her poetry is poorly written, that will be bad. She valued words more than nearly anything else. If it's excellent, that'll be worse, that she suffered as she did and had no communion. But can one box of stuff, scooped willy-nilly from the detritus of a house, represent a life in any meaningful way?

I open the box, finally. Now I am opening the box. I am setting my laptop aside to find the box in order to open it.

{ 2 }

My friend Frenchy, who'd been my boss when I was a young military diver in the 1980s and who'd done two tours in the war, returned to Vietnam with me in 1995. I was eager to show my mother the photographs. When I did, her head shook softly with palsy, no no no no no. We sat on a relative's couch—we couldn't very well sit in her house—as I asked questions, hoping she could tell me what I was looking at. But she'd already developed ways to mask memory loss.

"Oh gosh," she said each time. "I'll just have to think about it."

I'd come home too late.

I drove her to the house I despised and feared like a nightmare. She was frail in her dirty blue jacket, and it was like helping somebody's grandmother out of the car. My mother was old enough to be my grandmother. Of course there was no working light on the carport or in the back of the house. I love you, I said hopelessly in the near-dark. I love you too, she said and carefully, one step at a time, went up the stairs, walked through the door, and shut it behind her.

A house is a box filled with cushions to soften the blows. Hers sold, after she was taken from it, for less then $20,000, an investment with no return. I would have torn it down and started over.

{ 3 }

The absence of older generations is a freedom like the cold void of space, our little personalities struggling to keep warm as we sail along under our own flags, dodging asteroids, ice belts, and space pirates.

{ 1 }

We've moved across the country to take new jobs, and the house is a mess. I'm sure you'll forgive me for being unable to find the box I've been describing.

{ 2 }

Her irresponsibility made her something both greater and lesser. She coasted willfully through life with a kind of waggish dignity, but by the end she was tired. She almost seemed relieved that the Alzheimer's ward had an alarm on the door so no one could escape through the deadly deep corn.

{ 3 }

Young Master Hawkins sits on a hill overlooking the ocean, searching the combers for a longboat filled with tricorner hats. But it's not the pirates that you know are coming who get you. It's the ones in the chairs next to you now, the ones camped inside.

One of my first memories: my mother slapping me hard across the face. I was probably three or four, and it woke me into the world. She'd been wiping my mouth with a wet washcloth that had grown cold, and I tried to knock her hand away. Don't you *ever* hit a woman, she hissed. She'd been a teacher, and the slap was a lesson: see how things are.

One day, three or four years before I left home, she was angry about my leaving trash on the carport. I bent over to pick it up but smart-mouthed her doing it, and she beat my back with her belt. I stood up, taller now than she was, and laughed mutiny in her face. She burst into tears. See how things are.

{ 1 }

The story ends here: I got the call from my sister, who lived downstate, near the nursing home. My mother lay on her deathbed behind a curtain in a chilly Medicaid room. She was gaunt, body as wasted as her mind, but her face had smoothed somehow in the process, and she looked twenty years younger. I talked to her and held her hand. She was as calm, attentive, and interested as she'd been when I was a child. When I finished, she began to whisper to me, looking in my eyes. She spoke a long time. It was gibberish, there were no words left, but her speech rhythms were eloquent. It was clear to me, anyway, they were in service to atonement, blessing, love. A final gift, the map left behind in the trunk. Unscroll it and it's blank.

So this was the rise and fall of the American dream within two generations, and I'm left wondering: Am I ahead, behind, or dead even with my forebears? Am I box, loser, or pirate? Choices, choices.

{ 2 }

Having decided to become a pirate myself, I was expected to bury some treasure. She lay cold in a box in the mortician's basement while we picked clothes, music, and verses. He'd hung taxidermied heads on the paneled walls of his office. At the cemetery, listening to words I chose coming from a stranger's mouth, I held my firstborn son and stared at the casket, case closed. She was truly gone now, silent forever and unaccountable.

With my deep focus I realized suddenly I could see my mother's profile, through a narrow space between box and lid, where a gasket must have been missing. Her nose was like the beak of a bird of prey in silhouette against a strip of sunny grass on the other side of the family plot. I sat frozen in horror at my failure to conduct even the business of death properly, or at least to stop everything right then and there, to say something that would set things right. But I said nothing, and let's be realistic: the smiling worms will have us, no matter what we write or how we live.

{ 3 }

If the movies have taught us nothing else, it's that we will make a color-ful escape on the day of execution. Having outwitted the cell, we run and swing from a line dangling on the yardarm, meant to hang us ceremonially. Her Majesty's marines blast away uselessly at the sky; the governor looks down in his frills, incredulous and raging. We let go and free-fall into the sea, where our vessel, bluff-sterned, tall-masted, lies at anchor in the near distance. The captain of the garrison, a demigod, can't help but admire our spirit, even if he has been trying to kill us. He instructs his lieutenant to delay pursuit for a day, just to make things more sporting. The junior officer, like the mere mortal he is, goggles.

The horizon is the way out.

The way back in.

Edge of the known world.

Unemployed, in Greenland?

Four hundred years before the advent of the blog, the great English scholar Robert Burton wrote: "'Tis most true, [many have an incurable urge to write] . . . in this scribbling age. . . . Out of an itching humor that every man hath to show himself, desirous of fame and honor . . . he will write no matter what and scrape together it boots not whence."

My own itching humor has scraped together a lot of words these last years, much of which I published under the pen name Oronte Churm, a combination of two characters' names in a short story by Henry James that's about who or what is real in society, art, and human feeling. I invented a pen name to begin with because I believed it was necessary to protect my job and my family's well-being.

For a dozen years I taught in the English Department of what I call here Hinterland University, in a town I call Inner Station. It's a Big Ten flagship campus with enough very polite (mostly white, suburban) kids to form two or three infantry divisions, which most will never have to consider as employment.

My wife and I moved to Inner Station because she's a Hinterland alum and wanted her dream job in the study abroad office there. I'd just finished a later-in-life graduate degree in creative writing and was writing a novel. I asked for a job teaching undergrad rhetoric, creative writing, and literature, and became a lecturer at the university, *adjunct* faculty: "connected to a larger or more important thing"; "something added to but not essentially a part of the thing," as the dictionaries say. I taught more than tenured professors but was paid half, conditions similar to (or slightly better than) those of most contingent faculty in America who, along with grad students, now teach 75 percent of classes on college campuses for low pay, few benefits, and no job security.

The human-resources rep told me I needn't worry about signing up for state retirement. According to her, adjuncts were fired (by the euphemism of "contracts not renewed") after four years, so the state wouldn't be required to vest them in their plans. In this and other ways higher education in America has merely followed the larger corporate trend for outsourced and part-time labor. When I was hired, there were already some fifty adjuncts in HU's Department of English alone, and that number would nearly double.

Teaching is, generally, the best job I've ever had, and I've tried food service, snake handling, soldiering, house painting, bus driving, retail, graphic-arts production, advertising, and other things. I am never bored teaching, which counts for nearly everything with me. Most of us would just like to work at something fulfilling, to be compensated fairly, and to feel we'll be allowed to continue to do our jobs without unexplained or capricious layoffs.

I heard rumors of one rimy adjunct in the department who'd been there fifteen years. I cornered the assistant to the director of rhetoric in a bar and asked him how long I might really expect to keep my job if it turned out we stayed in town for a while. He was an older PhD candidate whom I liked and respected—he was the best teacher I've ever seen—and he would become an adjunct himself when his funding ran out.

He took a long drag off his smoke and said seriously, "As long as you aren't caught fucking a student . . . on your desk . . . during class . . . you'll never lack for work."

But the stocks in Hinterland's portfolio fell after 9/11, and a state budget crisis prompted the moneyman to whisper again in the provost's ear: "We must revert to an older model and get rid of all these people. Never mind if they're buying houses and raising children here; we warned them it wasn't real work. Put it to them like this: A compromised operating budget requires reduced reliance on adjunct labor by increasing class sizes to enormous lectures and offering fewer courses. . . ."

I'm sorry to say, for our students' sakes, that my friend in the bar, with his campus teaching awards and long experience, his good humor, wit, and institutional memory, had to find another job on campus when he could no longer get full-time work as a lecturer, and then he moved away. Many other adjuncts were let go in a series of purges, and others were hired to replace them, eventually. Like Ishmael at the end of *Moby-Dick*, I often found myself adrift and nearly alone on the heartless adjunct sea. As the novel's epilogue recalls, "And I only am escaped alone to tell thee."

Mostly, I didn't think overmuch about the political implications of any of this. I did my job enthusiastically and well, I believe—I too got the awards—did everything asked of me and volunteered for more, tried to be a good departmental citizen, published two books, and walked my kids home from school every day and started dinner. I was lucky.

Yet every so often, when I realized that the guys who mowed the grass on the quad were paid more than I was, or it was rumored another giant layoff was coming, I'd mount a comically towering rage and draft manifestos in my head:

> That our labor is often exploited is not the entire point. That the system has created a problem too big not to have catastrophic consequences if addressed now is not our concern. That there is harsh class division, with administrators and some professors on top and everyone else below, is typical. That this system—which purports to stand for self-realization, enlightenment, rationality, equity, democracy, human rights, and opportunities for all—is the one doing the exploiting is the real bite in the ass.

Burton says, "I did for my recreation now and then walk abroad, look into the world, and could not choose but make some little observation . . . sometimes again I was [an insolent derider], and then again [anger burned my liver]."

Our world invites observations too. And sometimes, when you think you have no agency, you must assemble your little pirate crew to storm the castle of privilege and power. Your assets? Not much, besides your own wits (not exactly rapier-like), what strength you can muster, and a new suit. Somehow, miraculously, you reach the base of the ivory towers.

Give us the key, you tell the gatekeeper, who is known for his heartlessness.

I have no key, he says.

Rip his arms off, you tell your giant.

Oh, you mean *this* key, the gatekeeper says.

〰

Things got pretty dicey for us in the middle years of that decade. My wife took what she thought was a better job on campus, but it was phased out quickly and there were no others to be had, even in the clerical pool. We had two children by then. I continued to teach and to apply for tenure-track jobs, which would have to be at some other university or college. Tenure hiring is a perpetual buyers' market, and with the economy gone south it was close to statistically impossible.

We talked about leaving, taking a chance, doing something else, making it an adventure, maybe even going abroad. But how far could we have gotten on what we had, and where would we have gone?

Those with power or resources have always blamed those without for their own misfortune. You hear bootstrap narratives in every recession and depression: Move to the big city, you lazy rube, where all the jobs are. Get a job as pool hustler so you can send the money home to Carterville.

Move from the urban jungle to the countryside, you slum dweller you, that's where they have all the jobs. Grow yourself some healthy fresh kumquats to mail to your family back there under the El tracks.

Make art from ruined plasterboard, clean the wealthy's tombstones, start a glove factory. Hopeless advice. The only thing those people really want for you to have is a sure sense of your own defeat.

My wife decided to do a master's in library science while I kept working, and eventually she got a rewarding new job in a middle school in town. Before that period was over we had accumulated a lot of debt, and our house badly needed work we couldn't afford. I have identified closely with people in the news who say they are one bad event from foreclosure.

Surely there's more than one kind of luck. Consider the Beatles.

That Paul met John at a garden fête in 1957 is something like fate. Sure, Liverpool was a relatively small city, and they were both interested in music, and scientists hadn't invented Internet addiction yet, which meant there was a somewhat less-than-impossible chance they'd meet. But it's not something Paul could have prepared for—a mutual friend who played tea-chest bass to spontaneously introduce them, that John wouldn't be jealous and prickly that day, or too drunk to remember fifteen-year-old Paul. That the event wouldn't be canceled due to rain. It's fun to play the game of Freak Yourself Out Over Things That Might Easily Not Have Been.

But there's another kind of luck, as in the story that says John gave Paul an ultimatum a few years later: Go on the road with me playing gigs for next to nothing, or stick around Liverpool to do trade work to your dad's plan. Me or your own father, in effect. The ultimatum, though coercive and maybe even sadistic, forced Paul to make a hard choice based on his understanding of his developing skills as a musician, John's charisma, Liverpool's traps, and the vision of Elvis in movies. We refer popularly to what happened after that as incredibly lucky, not just for Paul but for all of us. But it seems a lot less capricious, that fate, and more like semi-informed free will.

The first kind of luck is out of my control. Why wasn't I lucky enough to have been born to a father who was president of American Motors? Because few are. An op-ed in the *Post* quotes someone saying that Mitt Romney's "outsized wealth is the direct result of his own hard work at Bain Capital," and adds, "No one is claiming that Romney didn't earn his money or that he isn't a very hard worker."

I guess. But I've known some awfully hardworking people who didn't thrive, let alone become rich and powerful, including my own teacher mother, who raised me alone and spent her golden years in a washing machine factory, throwing rejects into a railroad car. I find the cultural blindness to the powerful's kind of "luck" astonishing, and of course it goes hand-in-hand with a different kind of bootstrap narrative, the "self-made man," an issue that became central in the most recent presidential-campaign furor over, and inquiry into, whose orifice, exactly, the silver spoon was inserted.

But I still believe in trying to prepare for the second kind of luck, all of us, by developing our capabilities according to interest, time, and resources— taking the bus across town to learn a new chord, as it were. It makes sense, if only to take on challenges that can make life interesting and rewarding. A lifelong revelation of self, to self, by immersion in a world not of one's own making: this used to be called education. The goal being not some corporate philosophy of "yield" but the hope for better things and perhaps more choices yet.

"An unexamined life is not worth living," Socrates says.

On the other hand, we know how that worked out for Socrates.

~~~

Two autumns ago, before the semester started at Hinterland, I went to West Virginia to get some writing done. There I had a dream. In the dream I inherited $125 million and was very happy. This seemed plausible because in waking life a distant relative once promised to leave me $125,000, which made me happy even though I knew I'd never see it.

In the dream I walked around my large house, which was being professionally and extensively renovated, and met groups of people I knew in different rooms. In the library I promised old friends we'd take an epic road trip together; in the kitchen I told Crazy Larry, an actor friend who works as a technology manager, that of course I'd put up a production of something he'd star in; in the foyer I snubbed a bunch of people I never liked anyway. It all felt so right, so good, so *true*.

Imagine my confusion when I woke in the pitch black on a swayback bed in the damp air up a short mountain in West Virginia. I lay there, maybe as long as a long minute, absolutely *sure* the dream had been real and this two a.m. darkness was false. When the brain, our selfsame organ, plays trickster, how are we to make sense of the parts of the world, let alone integrate them?

"Is all that we see or seem / But a dream within a dream?" Poe wonders.

Of all the talented, dedicated adjuncts I knew in a dozen years at Hinterland, I can think of only six who finally fell into what's called the tenure stream, though many had other successes. You can understand why I pinched myself, hard, when I got one of those jobs within a few months of my windfall dream.

The hiring university's state economy was in such a mess that the Governor Himself had to sign a special override to the hiring freeze, as I remember it. But suddenly I was an assistant professor at a long-running creative-writing program, where there was all the jambalaya and bread pudding in the world. It was as if the universe had rolled over and sighed, You know, it's just *not that hard*.

My family prepared to move from the Midwest to the Gulf Coast. We sold Churm House quickly and got a good price for it, another minor miracle in a bad economy. After that it did get harder, starting with how a multinational bank, paranoid from subprime problems of its own making, demanded things from us for two months that were often contradictory, impossible by their own rules, undefined, or repetitive, before it finally, lazily, deigned to give us a mortgage on a new house.

Technically, my family was homeless for five weeks during that time, though not on the street or in shelters. And we had resources, even if they were mostly credit cards. But we were hemorrhaging money for hotels—there were no house rentals available—and never knew if the end was even in sight. My mother-in-law, who moved with us, was very ill. My wife didn't have a new job yet. The kids weren't allowed to register for school, and we couldn't get a bank account because we had no local address. Our two cars looked like the Joads' truck and had to be emptied and repacked every time we moved to new housing.

To save ourselves financially we moved to an extended-stay place, the next town over, for unmarried men who work the rigs, refineries, and chemical plants. The rooms were . . . *tidied* each afternoon but not once cleaned, not even the toilets, and I played guessing games with my kids about what the kumquats on the walls and ceiling really were. Every morning I used the brush on the end of my ice scraper to wipe ash and soot from our minivan windows. Every night I cooked for five on the two-burner stove in the efficiency kitchen with its little fridge that wouldn't stay closed, sniffing food to try to determine if it had gone bad overnight.

I really was homeless for a time as a teen, and this was merely an uncomfortable reminder. But seeing my children in a semblance of risk did much worse things. My little Wolfie said hopefully at one point that we could all go to the mall to ride the escalators, since they were free, he was pretty sure. For this father, it's a quick ride on public transport from there to Eat the Rich.

Point is, even that place, the cheapest, grimiest, and furthest-flung of our paid sojourns, cost us a month's rent *every week*. What if I had not been a tenure hire, with supportive colleagues waiting for my family, but another unknown working at McDonald's or for a lawn-care service or as an adjunct with a 5/5 teaching load at three different colleges around town, for a total of $15,000? What if we had simply needed work of any kind, had heard there was work to be had, and made a leap of faith?

Finally a colleague stepped in and very generously donated a small but lovely in-town vacation home for our use. My boys splashed in the pool, our pets lay in sunlight pooled on the hardwood floor, and panic rose in my throat in the smell of calm affluence. Ten days later the bank got off its swollen ass and gave us the loan, but we didn't know whether it would go through until the day we closed.

In the end, the crazy-desirable opportunity my new position represented cost my family the equivalent of a nicely appointed new Ford Fiesta, a sum that went on credit cards after all the cash was gone. I couldn't have foreseen more than half of those costs, and that's exactly why "just move if you don't like your job" is, at one level, patently absurd.

Now of course we are, as I believe they say in the South, squatting in high cotton. But I'm constantly reminded of how many adjuncts are genuinely among the working poor in America, one of the shames of higher ed. Many lofty ideas are professed in the presence of disenfranchised contingent labor.

Am *I* happy, now that I have everything I could want?

~~~

At home I dream that at Naples, at Rome, I can be intoxicated with beauty, and lose my sadness. I pack my trunk, embrace my friends, embark on the sea, and at last wake up in Naples, and there beside me is the stern fact, the sad self, unrelenting, identical, that I fled from. I seek the Vatican, and the palaces. I affect to be intoxicated with sights and suggestions, but I am not intoxicated. My giant goes with me wherever I go.

—RALPH WALDO EMERSON

~~~

The pay and title are better, the worries and stresses have changed, but my interests remain: What does it mean to be educated? To think and write well? In that I'll continue to do what I've always tried to do: help students to see and to express themselves better, even as I try to help myself do the same.

But of course that's a lifelong journey, its gains always temporary and therefore comic. Picture Long John Silver, at the end of the film *Treasure Island*, his dory filled with stolen gold, rowing and sinking; rowing, sinking, and gloating.

~~~

When I reread these pieces pulled from the hundreds of thousands of words I've published as Churm, they look like grapplings from the tangle of my thoughts about class, work, fatherhood, the natural world, and the written word. Pulled dripping into view, scraped of barnacles, they compose a sort of memoir, one salvaged from earnest attempts to see if I knew anything at all. Are they representative?

What sea of ideas is contained in our vellum skins?

The Art of War

Coal from the mines in southern Illinois burned dirtier than western coal, so my hometown grew slowly poorer, decade by decade, after the high-production years around World War I. Back then my grandfather was an international organizer for the United Mine Workers of America, a sub-district union president, and a state senator, the kind of man who intended to buy an entire city block so he could install his four grown children in homes around his own. They'd be a working-class American dynasty, and he would take care of everyone. My mother was the youngest of four children and was always "Baby" to him and he "Daddy" to her, and my earliest notions of manhood were based on his rise to beneficent power from such a rough start.

He managed only to get a mail-order certificate from the Miners' and Mechanics' Institute, but he sent my mother to Stephens College, where Joan Crawford had gone briefly. A couple of our older citizens still remember my mother as a beautiful young woman in a convertible, breezing into town from some new adventure. She worked as a secretary for *Life* and taught in Florida. She married twice—three times if you count the short-lived secret marriage to a common foot soldier in World War II, which Daddy got annulled. He also wouldn't let her join the Women Airforce Service Pilots, or WASPs, so she got her private pilot's license to spite him, and it was reported in the newspaper. She went back for a master's degree, spoke some French, and loved it when Jackie Kennedy asked André

Malraux to the White House. When I was very small, she still dressed stylishly around the house and was perfumed with Chanel Nº5.

As you can imagine, she had a complicated relationship with the miners, shopkeepers, and factory workers whose children were in her classroom. Her Daddy died in 1948, a victim of his pipe and the poisons of the mines he'd started in as a boy. With him gone the family lost influence, and her own fortunes began to fail. No doubt some townsfolk thought she had a superiority complex with no basis in reality. But southern Illinois was her home, and she knew and identified with the people better than some may have realized. Like them, she took pride in being hard when necessary—she was "both mother and father" to me, she said—and I think some understood that about her.

The barbershop she took me to was downtown, in the same building as the Western Union office that was also a toy shop, a candy store, and a Greyhound bus terminal. The owner had been the town's scoutmaster for so many years that he'd taken boys to see Red Grange, the Galloping Ghost, play ball at the University of Illinois, and when their flivver boiled over coming home, he had his scouts run relays down to a creek by the road, scoop water in their hats, and pour it in the radiator as he kept driving along, slowly. The building wasn't air-conditioned, as I remember, and the old wooden floors creaked when you walked from one business to the other. The giant transom over the shared door was always open, so the toy shop smelled of talc and drowsy warm lather, and the barbershop rang with register bells and phone calls from next door.

There were two barbers. One was squat and greased his hair back flat. The other was thin and bald. I was about five and thought of them as old, old men, but they were surely only in their early fifties. My mother asked them if she could leave me to wait my turn while she ran next door to the cobbler. Other men waited in metal armchairs in the heat. I was almost never around men. My dad was gone, and most of my close relatives were women. I didn't want her to go but was too afraid to cry. The barbers laughed and said sure, they'd take care of me alright and to take her time; I was going to be just fine. My mother told me to be good and to listen to them and walked out.

The thin barber, who rarely spoke—he had a kind, patient grandpa voice, or so I imagined, since all my grandparents were dead—asked me to climb up on a booster seat on the big swivel chair. As he was tightening the shroud around my neck, one of the loafers reading a magazine said something, and the stocky barber said he'd get his turn, they'd be done with me in two shakes. He stropped a razor on a wide leather belt and went to work on the man in his own barber's chair.

"Nice lady," he said in a strong tenor. "Her father was an important man."

"Mm-hm," his partner replied, cutting my hair with scissors.

"And such a big boy. How old are you getting to be now, son? Soon you'll be all grown up."

When they saw I was too shy to speak, they started the talk among themselves that my mother had interrupted. I didn't know what the Tet Offensive was, but it interested me when a customer read things aloud from the paper about Marines dying. I knew about soldiers and war, from the TV show *Combat!* Both the barbers, I believe, had been Marines in the Pacific, the stocky one at Corregidor and the thin quiet one at Bataan. Could that much bad luck have been in one room? It was the first time I heard the phrase "death march." They talked about atrocities and the dead they knew or had seen. Someone said life was cheap in Asia and we'd have worse problems in Vietnam soon, same it went on all those islands.

"I never thought of the Japanese as anything more than animals," someone said. "It was easy to kill 'em. And I didn't do this, but I know a guy, one of my friends, who's still got a jar of Jap ears he pickled in GI gin. He keeps them in the pantry at home. Look just like canned mushrooms."

"Hope his wife never gets them confused," another man said. There were chuckles.

The room was silent as the grandfatherly barber held me by the shoulder with his thin strong fingers and scraped a blade down the back of my neck.

The stocky barber spoke up again. "Another Marine I know mailed himself all the parts of a .50 caliber machine gun. He's still got it oiled up and ready to go in his attic, twenty-five years later. Scary thing is, he's not all there. That gun could wipe out a *town*."

My mother returned and the shop went silent except for the thin barber, who told her how good I'd been. She thanked and paid him. I held her hand as we walked down the sidewalk under the awnings toward the fabric store she loved but which burned my nose and throat with its chemical odor.

"Learn anything good?" she asked, looking down at me.

Did she know? She smiled.

The Expulsion of
Oronte Churm

My final duty station as an army diver was the Republic of Panama. Our detachment lived on Fort Kobbe, the tiny army post on Howard Air Force Base, outside Panama City. We were attached to an engineer company but spent most of our time working independently from them in the canal or Gatun Lake or Portobello Bay. Sometimes we went to the jungle with the airborne infantry battalion that lived across the street or cross-trained with Special Forces. It was good duty, with two warm oceans full of living reefs, and smart, creative people who could have been doing just about anything but had volunteered, three or four times over, to be military frogmen and deep-sea divers.

I joined the service to get the money for college. In my era it was called VEAP, Veterans Educational Assistance Program, to differentiate it from the free ride that the GI Bill had been since World War II. Still, the government put in two dollars to my one, and after I had saved a set amount there was a bonus, and the total would be enough to get me through a state school after I got out. I achieved that financial goal when my original three-year enlistment was up, but I re-upped for an additional year to get the chance to go to Panama with my team and open the dive section there.

There were even more adventures to be had in army diving after a tour in Panama—Korea, Germany, and later, all over the world—and Frenchy, who'd left diving to become a command sergeant major by then, begged me to stay in. I agreed to do so, thinking I'd take it a year at a time. But when I talked to the reenlistment NCO, he played a sales game with me and said

I'd have to reenlist for four years or nothing. He couldn't do anything about that, he said; it was the way the system worked. I told him I'd think about it and walked straight to the education office on Kobbe to get some help with college applications. Frenchy went to the command headquarters on Fort Clayton and talked to them about the recruiter. They said I was welcome to re-up for any length of time I saw fit, but I'd already decided on what I was calling freedom.

The educational office on Fort Kobbe was, like everything else, housed in a multistory colonial building with a red tile roof. Most of the common areas and hallways in the buildings were open to the tropical breeze; bedrooms and some offices were air-conditioned behind closed doors. This office was usually locked. A bulletin board in the hallway held a few humidity-wrinkled, fly-specked sheets announcing a limited selection of beginning college classes, across the isthmus, and extension degree programs through, I think, the University of Maryland. They were impossible for soldiers whose jobs took them to the field regularly, but that's the way it was. I had to return several times before I found a "counselor" on duty.

I really had only one question: Did I have to list the community college courses I'd taken several years earlier on my college apps? My good intention was to get a fresh start; I wanted to take the courses over again as refreshers and wouldn't try to claim the credits. Anyway, I had another course of study in mind. The counselor said to leave them off my applications.

A couple of years into my undergraduate studies at NHSU-Tundra, my advisor, an older professor who would soon become the English Department head, asked where I had learned what he called my "whorehouse Spanish," and all this came out. He got excited for me and said I must get the old community college transcripts to him, so I could transfer those credits and get my degree done more quickly. If I was going to get anywhere in life, I must learn to work the system, he said; I was doing magnificently with my studies, and he was thrilled that I was an officer in the English honor fraternity, but I had to see to my career.

Shortly afterward some administrative computer processed my request, and I was expelled from the university. My crime was falsifying my original application by not listing every institution of higher learning that I'd attended. I was invited, in the letter I received, to reapply to the university, if there were any excuses for what I'd done. I would be given thirty days to do so.

I had no connections or help to enlist on my side, other than my embarrassed advisor, who now seemed to want to avoid the matter. The father of my girlfriend at the time, a therapist and school counselor in a wealthy Chicago suburb, and a former Marine, offered to help but was so indignant for me that I feared he might do something rash. I told him I'd go it alone, and I wrote the letter and sang the *mea culpas*. I was given an audience with the dean of Liberal Arts and Sciences.

A straight wind of at least twenty-five miles per hour always sweeps through the town of Tundra. That day the hot gusts were enough to knock pedestrians off their feet. The dean had my letter in her hand in her cool office but made me tell the story again. Then, after a dramatic pause, and in a tone that suggested the taste in her mouth from such a bad egg, she deigned to absolve me: "I see several dozen cases like this every year, Mr. Churm," she said. "You are the first to be readmitted to this university. I had better not hear your name again until it's time for you to walk across the stage and take the diploma from my hand. Go." She pointed her finger at the door.

I was relieved and got in my pickup that still had Department of Defense stickers on it and drove several hours to my girlfriend's home, where her parents took us for an expensive meal in a fish house. My income came from VEAP checks and a job at a gas station, where I was the only cashier not yet robbed at gunpoint.

I reviewed the fields of linen with their silver in rank-and-file and their blood-dark tulips of wine. What a lucky boy am I, I thought, to be allowed to continue my education.

Tenacity

Ceci n'est pas une histoire d'un pigeon.

One night in Hanoi, before official U.S. rapprochement with Vietnam, Frenchy and I were in the Piano Restaurant and Bar awaiting the house special—Roasted Pigeon with Five Tastes. Frenchy wanted the dish, he said, because he didn't think they could do it.

We were exhausted from a month of backpacking, and I was sick with what I can only describe as sinking spells, brought on by the strange rain-mist in northern Vietnam the French called *crachin*, which my dead grand-mother would have called "pneumonia weather." Our brains were saturated with an antimalarial drug that caused psychotic episodes in some users, and both of us were feeling odd.

(Before we left on our trip, I was out jogging long after dark and came up behind someone with a guitar case, walking in the road. We were a mile out of town, and it was sleeting. He was six feet tall, but somehow I knew he was a leprechaun and was afraid to look at his face as I passed. Thinking on it, I'm sure it was the mefloquine. Why would a leprechaun have a mullet?)

Frenchy and I drank beer and watched workers in gray coveralls, just outside the open doors of the restaurant, lift a sewer cover in the street with a pry bar, lower pails on long hemp ropes, and pull up gallon after gallon of night soil for the fields. As they poured the muck into a waiting cart, the stink bloomed.

Now the waiter arrived with the silver tray. He bent, smiled, and lifted the serving cover. The Pigeon with Five Tastes lay flattened on its dish like a bird accidentally cleated into a soccer pitch. Its back was broken, head thrown back, and beak open wide in a silent squawk of agony. It might have had a better plucking. We thighed the squab, and it collapsed under the weight of the blade into the puddle of its muddy gravy. Across the room an old woman played the theme to *The Godfather* on the eponymous piano, last tuned for Emperor Bao Dai, as her daughter tortured a violin.

Frenchy took a bite. "I don't know about *five* tastes," he said. "I don't like the one I'm gettin'. It's not even a good *smell*."

A few shreds of meat, dark and slick, stuck to the jackstraw bones. I gave up and finished my rice, but Frenchy bent over the plate and probed the corpse for sustenance.

"Listen, this is an old bird," he said. "He must have run a long way before they finally caught him."

He pried at the bones with knife and fork then sucked gristle from the wing tendons.

"I'm trying," he said, sounding confused. He wiped his forehead with a greasy napkin. "I swear to God I keep tryin' and tryin' to eat this thing. . . ."

Tenacity is not all virtue, and the more difficult the task, the more we invite judgment on our efforts. The problem is revealed in the etymology of the word: it comes from the Latin *tenere*, to hold. The metaphor connects holding on and its reward, naturally enough, but it's easy for tenacious people to look ridiculous.

Some find the tenacity needed to teach comical. We keep tryin' and tryin', meeting infrequently for just an hour at a time, to profess things to a diverse and often large audience, who may not have had enough interest in the subject to look into it on their own, and who, over the previous twelve to sixteen years of their educational lives, may have developed an antipathy to schedules, textbooks, the English language, teachers who remind them of their plumber fathers, and the screech of chalk on slate.

Every time students catch sight of us coming through the door, they examine us as if we are exotic moths lured with acetylene lamps on a moonless night, judging, measuring, classifying, and pinning us to the board as *types*.

They make me out to be the sardonic Kevin Spacey *type*, their evaluations say, the Geoffrey Rush/Woody Allen type, the knock-kneed, humpbacked, pigeon-toed, google-eyed, snaggletoothed, potbellied, baldheaded, chicken-necked, horse-faced *type* who tries to sell them on the brilliance of literary stories while the sun shines and bees buzz in the begonias. It takes tenacity—and several class meetings—to dissolve their quick judgments. (Sometimes, for effect, I used to stop discussions at Hinterland and have them consider my competition: the strangled cry of Reverend Jimmy, an itinerate charismatic who roosted on the quad and crowed himself hoarse about "sorority hoors and their fornicaturrs.")

It's human to pigeonhole, but as the tacitly mature one in this artificial relationship of teacher and students, I have obligations they do not, so I try to remember that perceptions change with context and experience. The students I taught at La Universidad de Cuba Libre a decade ago were generally very different from those at Hinterland.

But at the start of the fall semester, forced to wear long pants for the first time since April and reminded that I'm so shy that I faint if other shoppers stare at me when the butcher calls my number, I'd forget all that and greet the newest murder of undergrads as generic types.

At the top of the grade scale would be one or two Buddy Fasttracks, for whom the game of institutional education came easy. Most Buddies were the real thing; they had other interests, ambitions, even brilliance, and would take their drives and talents out of the academy when given the chance. But some were so narrowly focused that they couldn't, as Frenchy would say, pour the piss out of a boot if the instructions were written on the heel. And while I relied on their zeal for class discussions, I had to work hard to balance it with their peers' desire to strangle them.

The mass of students I saw at Hinterland led lives of quiet desperation. The university attracted the best of the really-very-good students in the state, but if they could have gotten into or paid for Harvard or Berkeley, most would have gone there. They were expected to go to college by their entire middle-class suburban culture and were dutifully doing just that, for the reasons told them: getting an education meant greater lifetime earnings, and besides, Zane, if your Uncle Tommy can get a degree, anybody can for christ's sake. They took notes and looked thoughtful when my facial expressions and tone cued thoughtfulness but were often bemused by readings such as Harlan Ellison's story "The Man Who Rowed Christopher Columbus Ashore," a metafictional story-in-fragments that's ethically difficult but suggests mediocrity is a sin.

On the whole, the Unwashed Middle would have been happier (and might have benefitted more from) falling in love to the trumpeting of elephants in the Barcelona Zoo or pouring concrete in lower Alabama, but if they ever wanted other experiences they had agreed to defer them (sometimes forever) in order not to suffer the indignities of, and very real financial penalties for, not finishing the bachelor's degree they were expected to start. These students would get A-minuses and B-pluses, and I would write many of them recommendation letters based on their "reliability" and "solidity."

On the lower end of the curve were those who rebelled in the most conventional, passive ways possible: they pulled Tommy Hilfiger hoodies over their heads, clacked tongue studs on their chipped front teeth, and looked pained. Out of ten such students, nine would put in the seat time (at the back of the room) to collect diplomas. Four would tape the words "HI MOM" to the top of their mortarboards at commencement, and two (both male) would perform rehearsed fist-pumps as they walked across stage to signal their accomplishment.

I keep trying, as a teacher, to make my thinking as sound as the good writing I espouse, which is, after all, a linear form: we follow type across the page as obediently as bird dogs. Yet life is one damn thing after another—running shoes and orange juice and that guy who looked at me funny—and the classroom becomes a dense cloud of impressions and perhaps-facts that I shape any way I can—chronologically, emotionally, narratively, rhetorically. It's those frantic grabs at meaning that can cause problems.

Sure, students fit categories, but none is really like another. If I could summon the strength to hold many facts before me at once, I might begin to see more clearly. But what to make of these student types?

(1) Janet was an apple-cheeked sophomore with the hair of Eva Braun. She insisted I call her Crow and filled her class journal with dark fantasies, such as the depiction of my murder in class and students standing around my corpse wondering if they should call the police. There was

a long appreciation on the shape of my skull in her response to Guy de Maupassant. The cover of the journal was heavily doodled—Crow announced she was "creative"—with pentagrams, Japanese animation characters, flowers, hearts, and the title "Not Satan's Notebook." Crow lurked behind corners to surprise me with questions and liked to loom over me in the pajamas she wore to class as I sat trapped in my chair. But she read thoughtfully, defended characters who were marginalized, and began to write coherently once I got her "creative" nature channeled. The last time I saw Crow she was sitting in the middle of the hallway in the English Department. She had upgraded her wardrobe to jeans and a Hawaiian shirt, but she was still drawing, this time a portrait of George Orwell with demented eyes. She stopped me to apologize for being (flutter hands wildly) back then.

(2) Jerry was polite and well spoken. He gobbled assigned literature as if starved for it, then asked for more. But he wrote short stories about girls so heavy they made Jell-O in the cafeteria tremble as they approached, and about foreigners in his dorm who stunk everything up. When I questioned this worldview in my written comments and suggested empathy as a path to revision, Jerry came to office hours in his WWJD wristband and shouted me down. Later, he worked as hard on his portfolio as any student I've had. I hesitated when he asked me to supervise his independent study senior year, the revision of a *bildungsroman* he had drafted in high school, presumably filled with scenes of the obese and the garlic-loving, narrated by a young hero keen on Jesus.

(3) Mo, a self-professed gangbanger in the Leveled Field program, when asked what subculture he might study for his ethnography assignment, replied, "Pimps or millionaires." His peers had chosen field sites such as the Frisbee Golf Club and the Pi Kappa Alpha house, so I was down for his originality. But since he couldn't drive long distances to a big city several times a week, I had to ask if pimps or millionaires congregated in Inner Station. My question was discouragement enough for the fierce young man to disengage and fail the course.

Gertrude Stein had an interest in cataloging human types. "I began to be sure," Stein said, "that if I could only go on long enough and talk and hear and look and see and feel enough and long enough I could finally describe really describe every kind of human being that ever was or is or would be living."

The problem, she found, as she became mired in writing *The Making of Americans*, was that while every person might be a type, every type was unique, and it would take infinite lifetimes to record all the specific characteristics of uncountable types: "I found that as often as I thought and had every reason to be certain that I had included everything in my knowledge of any one something else would turn up that had to be included."

It was an "endlessly interesting" problem to her, but "I went on and on and then one day after I had written a thousand pages . . . I just did not go on any longer."

Stein's difficulties are those of thoughtful people of all ages and chosen professions. To see people—life itself—with any degree of clarity takes time, courage, and tenacity.

⌣⌣⌣

It's night in Hanoi, and raining again. A murderer in canvas shoes pads down an ancient stone alley behind Dong Xuan Market. His hands are those of a strangler—fingers like rebar, rusty with nicotine and five-spice powder. He flicks the simple latch, opens the screen door. Come, little brother, he coos. His victim sits just out of reach. Birds flutter and panic. The killer doesn't want to be out here; he's getting wet, and his cigarette is smoldering, but he holds down his impatience in order to get the job done. The pigeon shifts uneasily from foot to foot, sidles to a far corner. Still, the man is tenacious; he knows the one he wants. Chef makes a grab, but the bird coyly eludes him, like a feathery little truth.

Crocodiles

I like stories about shifting impressions. In Chekhov's "The Lady with the Dog," Gurov returns home after a quick affair at a resort, and everything is beautiful:

> He returned to Moscow on a fine frosty day, and when he put on his fur-lined overcoat and thick gloves, and sauntered down Petrovka Street, and when, on Saturday evening, he heard the church bells ringing, his recent journey and the places he had visited lost their charm for him. He became gradually immersed in Moscow life, reading with avidity three newspapers a day, while declaring he never read Moscow newspapers on principle. Once more he was caught up in a whirl of restaurants, clubs, banquets, and celebrations, once more glowed with the flattering consciousness that well-known lawyers and actors came to his house, that he played cards in the Medical Club opposite a professor. He could once again eat a whole serving of Moscow Fish Stew in a pan.

I don't even like chowder, but that fish stew served in a pan makes me crazy with hunger. Contrast that scene with Gurov's impression of the very same place and people, just three paragraphs later. His rage is comic:

> What savage manners, what people! What wasted evenings, what tedious, empty days! Frantic card-playing, gluttony, drunkenness, perpetual talk always about the same thing. The greater part of one's time and energy went on business that was no use to anyone, and on discussing the same thing over and over again, and there was nothing to show for it all but a stunted wingless

existence and a round of trivialities, and there was nowhere to escape to, you might as well be in a madhouse or a convict settlement. (Garnett translation)

Chekhov writes the prose equivalent of Monet's paintings. After a while, you begin to see that variations of mood and tone—not haystacks or water lilies or card players or fish stew—are the real subject.

~~~

Mrs. Churm fell twice when she was pregnant with Starbuck, from a combination of inner-ear disturbance, shifting center of balance, and "ligament laxity," a loosening of the joints caused by new hormonal levels. The first time, she slipped on our front stairs, and we rushed to the hospital to see the midwife on duty.

Davie was a thin, low-talking Englishman with a ginger ponytail and a closely cropped beard. He was married and had his own kids, whom he took cycling and rock-climbing, and he volunteered at a shelter for at-risk pregnant teens. The only male midwife at our hospital, he wore a button on his scrubs that read, "Listen to the woman." He knew all about women's bodies and what would happen to them, while all I knew was enough to get us to this point. There was a group of former patients called "Davie's Girls" who gushed over him as if they were in junior high and he was the resident hottie.

Davie sent us for an ultrasound, checked Mrs. Churm inside and out, stripped off his gloves, washed up, and sat on a rolling stool directly in front of her. Speaking so softly that I had to strain to be included, he explained to her how a fall could shear the placenta from the uterine wall and starve the baby of food and oxygen.

"But really," he assured my wife, "you seem to be fine. Anyway, it's so early, it's not like we could take heroic measures."

Because I'm deeply in touch with my feelings, I can tell you that I was above all terrified for my wife and unborn child. I was also grateful to the point of tears for Davie's care and honesty. And when he said so matter-of-factly that my son wasn't viable I felt some evil crocodile rise from the swamp of my brain until its snaky eyes were just visible above the gray matter. It thought: You'll *pay* for that comment, you ponytailed *son of a bitch*.

~~~

It was a damp, drizzly semester in my soul. The young men were in love with violence. One said in class that he was getting aroused just thinking about actress Jennifer Garner punching him in the face. A young woman lectured us that no one had ever given birth alone; she knew this because her mom was an ob-gyn. My impressions of students had begun their slide back around the holidays, even as I rationalized that they had their own competencies, were athletes and future chemical engineers and captains of finance. I began to worry that this was all like a date that had gone on too long.

There are some professors—one in a departmental generation, maybe—who ripen and become happier and more generous the longer they're around the institution. They seem to have the good luck not to die of virulent cancers the year after they retire, and you see them in the hallways, busy but engaged with others' research, families, and lives. One I know reminds me of a black-and-white photo of poet-doctor William Carlos Williams in old age, laughing joyously under a dogwood in full blossom. I wanna become *that* guy.

~~~

The second time my wife fell, she did a full-on belly flop on the tile floor at her water-aerobics class. She was about a week shy of full term. I was horrified at what that kind of overpressure might do to the baby, but at the hospital they hooked her up to a belly band and a fetal monitor, and everything seemed fine.

Davie was the midwife on duty when Mrs. Churm finally went into labor. It was a slow night in labor and delivery. We also had in attendance a midwifery resident, a battle-ax nurse, which I mean in the most grateful and admiring way, and a doula we'd hired, so there was plenty of attention. I walked Mrs. Churm up and down the halls, pushed against her spine to counter back labor, and helped her in and out of showers. But when she went into the stage called transition, the most intense part of labor, when women lose their minds and so do their husbands, she was in the birthing-suite toilet. Davie sat on the floor at her feet, slumped against the wall, twirling his ponytail with one finger.

"I'm dying!" cried Mrs. Churm.

"Nooo, you're not," Davie said in a bored drone.

"I am! I am! I *am* dying!" Mrs. Churm cried. "Ohhhh . . ." Her groans were more horrible than her cries.

I excused myself, saying I'd just step out and eat my breakfast in the next room, since we'd been up twenty-four hours and I'd need my strength for the actual delivery. No one listened. I went out and bit into the gooey institutional muffin they'd brought on the breakfast tray. The crown stuck to the roof of my mouth in a big chocolate glob I couldn't chew, and I sobbed on top of what was left.

〰

Impressions change easily. Just when I was feeling most tired and a bit fed up, my student Madeline came to office hours. Her roommate had tried to kill herself, and the university had utterly failed everyone involved, leaving Madeline to care for this girl she didn't even know and whose mother wouldn't help, either. Madeline had written a short story that was miraculous in its ability to show the pain and confusion of recent weeks without self-pity or even anger at all those who'd let her down.

We'd just finished conferencing when I heard the disorganized noises that mark some violence, and a girl screamed, "Oh my god!" There were half a dozen teaching assistants, instructors, and lecturers in my group office, and maybe fifteen students.

As I jumped off my chair and rounded a tall bookcase I expected to see two guys scuffling on the floor. Instead, a young woman was thrown backward in grand-mal seizure on a teacher's desk. Her fellow students quickly lifted her feet off the floor and lay her flat, then formed a wall so she couldn't fall off. Even as I called 911 on my cell, another student a few feet away was speaking calmly to a dispatcher, and the police told me to hang up.

The girl thrashed and thrashed, fighting the thing that had her, and tears ran into her hair. She was rigid, silent, and perfectly white. Then she turned blue, and bright-red blood trickled down her chin. It wasn't like watching someone die; it was like looking at Death. But the students didn't back away. Two spoke loudly but reassuringly to her as others held her on the desk, and one young man—classmate, not boyfriend—stroked her head. I asked them to turn her on her side, and when they did she gasped loudly for breath. Someone shouted, "She's back!"

Her face turned cherry-red then from the buildup of carbon dioxide, and when her eyes opened they were totally pink from blown capillaries. She struggled to speak and rise but made no sense. I found myself saying loudly, "Stay down, sweetheart," not even knowing where that came from; a second later I realized I'd been speaking as if to one of my little boys and had to walk away. It was startling to acknowledge to myself that I'd begun to relate to my students as a father might. The paramedics were there by then, and in half an hour she was able to walk out with them. Her peers stayed with her the entire time. How had they become so strong and compassionate?

〰

Starbuck was born healthy. After I cut the cord they suctioned his airway, cleaned him, weighed him, and put him under the heater to pink up. Meanwhile Mrs. Churm was bleeding much too heavily.

Even Davie seemed flustered. He had a tray of instruments that included a curved needle that looked like it belonged to a sailmaker, and he was going to use it as soon as they could get the placenta to deliver. He roughly, impatiently, kneaded my wife's abdomen, and she cried out from pain sharper than anything that had come before. They gave her a shot that caused more contractions, and that was even more agonizing. When the placenta delivered, it came so fast that Davie didn't have his basin ready. I caught a glimpse of something as organic as lungs, and there was a hard liquid slap on the floor.

"Oh! Muh shoes!" Davie cried, and I knew everything would be OK.

〰

The details of what happened at Virginia Tech emerged slowly, but what has stayed with me ever since those first accounts is how Professor Liviu Librescu, seventy-six, a Holocaust survivor, held his classroom door shut long enough for a few students to jump from second-story windows to safety. I suspect that events happened so fast that his power to hold back Death as long as he did, before being killed, came from a deep and primitive feeling: These are *my* kids, you *son of a bitch*.

What a beautiful old crocodile.

Killing Pirates

I'd painted Starbuck's nursery with blue skies and a mural with a smiling monkey and an elephant he named Peanut. But now he was three and wanted cars and trucks and monsters and policemen for his new bedroom. And and and.

We compromised on pirates, but then he saw the Wyeth illustrations for *Treasure Island*, which bring to life "heavy, nut-brown" men with "dirty, livid white" scars, hands "ragged with black, broken nails," greasy hair, pistols, a cutlass, and a gold tooth glinting in a sneer.

Starbuck said precociously, "Pirates might be a little scary. Maybe when I get older." He still wanted boats, maps, and the swelling sea. *Treasure Island*, that is, minus Long John Silver and Captain Flint. His world was no longer only additive conjunctions.

My mother died that spring, and we wondered what to do about our little boy. Mrs. Churm regretted that her mother sheltered her from death. She didn't attend a funeral until she was fifteen. But I recalled being a child in the stench of lilies, a dank room with the cold focus up front and an audience of strange faces. The director crept along the walls like a rat.

We compromised, took him to the visitation to meet all the estranged kin and old ladies who read of it in the paper. He was to stay at the back of the room but wailed and stomped and demanded to see for himself.

I picked him up, and together we went forward to gaze at the frail corpse and the casket saddle made of stargazers, wood ferns, roses, and star grass the color of unbleached muslin. He was interested, solemn, and asked the proper questions: Is that Grandma Helen's body, is there a heaven, is Maggie the golden retriever with Grandma Helen and Grandpa Fred? Can we drive to heaven? Please? Will Grandma float in the air, will you die, will I die? Why?

The day was long—grandma but not Grandma, family but sadness, intense but boring. Starbuck butterflied around, fell down steps—twice—ate his hamburger and mine, and yelled that a Memorial Day parade was passing.

Rest easy, my mother loved collage: pallbearers watching baton-twirlers; Catholic friends arriving late with leftover Mardi Gras beads from their float and a pair of Groucho glasses for Starbuck. He put them on and insisted we admire him. The flag of death, so jolly with its eyelids and lips glued shut, hung stiffly on the mast.

At the cemetery, the little flirt sat in back with my nieces. We called him forward at the end, and he obeyed. I picked him up.

"Goodbye, Grandma," he said and waved to the coffin. He looked concerned that my shaking might not be laughter but was afraid to ask.

Then, as we drove away through the graveyard, he wanted to know if there were bones under all those stones.

"I want to see them," he demanded. "Can I see them? Please?"

My wife, looking at me, told him to stop it, and I said it was okay.

The unspeakable courage of a three-year-old boy slingshotting Blackbeard Death.

I Didn't Know

A white marble statue the size of a cat, demure as a cat, squats on a shelf by an east window, smiling under dust and the ink my childish pen traced in its contours.

Cracked with water-swollen wedges from one of five stone mountains (the one they call "Heaven"), carved with an iron adze and chisels by a craftsman at Non Nuoc, it sits now, amused, surrounded by my son's Babar, Nessie, George, Elmo, and a Harrod's bear in a Guard's bearskin hat.

I didn't know for a long time that my mother bought the little statue in Ben Thanh in 1963, expatriated it to southern Illinois locked in a cabinet of wonder the size of a coffin that also held old leis, a tiger-skin pocketbook, a concubine's wooden headrest, a Thai Ramayana rubbing of a demon seducing a maiden, a junk made of the amber and ebony horn of water buffalo, silk kimonos for man and wife.

A thousand petit treasures in the trunk, amid other clutter in the closed-off bedroom with her other curations: a grocery sack of my Kodachrome father (gone), chintz china of my father's mother (dead), the treadle Singer of her own mother (dead), the horsehair blanket her Daddy (dead) lay across his lap in his Ford motorcar. All the exotic dry rot without context or catalog, jewel-headed insects in a black widow's web.

She smiled when I begged to see, pleased at my interest, happy to help me hold ivory chopsticks, proud to tell old stories, how Vietnamese on the street asked to touch my sister's golden hair, how her maid Phuong, a clever girl but confused, had asked, "Madame want soup? Madame want soap?"

My mother served all memories, savory, sweet, or bitter, equally. How a man in the market had had his nose cut off by Communists, you could see into his skull; how the Saigon nurses couldn't contain their pleasure that I was born a boy; how she was there when Thich Quang Duc immolated himself in protest; that the human body, anyone, everyone, melts like butter if there's enough heat, she said. I didn't know that about democracy.

Oh, people are all alike, she assured me. Old Man Poorson in his market on our street (where I bought firecrackers she forbade) cheated his people on loaves of bread—let alone meat! Pulpit penitents, tears running down their cheeks—all cheating bastards, she said, those men bawling in church on Sunday (while my friends and I giggled over new lyrics to old hymns) and balling their secretaries Monday noon in the Herrin Motel. She didn't much care for the manager of Woolworth's either but made me apologize to him when I stole a little View-Master Jesus on a keychain. If you held it to the sun, He gazed upon you. I was four, and my cheeks burned from it. She smiled down at me with compassion and mercy.

My mother made me laugh, impressions of a schizophrenic cousin, doing the bickering voices; hulking across our living room like a local boor, my school's principal; her mimicking wheedle-dee-dee of the American consul in Saigon, who counseled with the voice of Slim Pickens to return home to our compound near Ton Son Nhut after my father tried to slap me from her arms.

The bull dyke who lived next to us in Saigon, a woman ex-Marine, no b.s. there, boy, she told me she would have whacked your father in the head with a Griswold cast-iron skillet while he slept.

I didn't know that so my mother told me and we laughed.

She smiled when she packed me off to show-and-tell at Bible camp with her white marble Buddha, a rare appearance for the little guy, in on the joke I didn't yet get. Her Daddy had been an alderman in that church, but my mother resigned as secretary due to their complete and total hypocrisy, jerks who looked down on a single mother when it was your father the one ran off with that whore. Now hurry or you'll miss it entirely. As long as it was on the way, we drove past that woman's house to see was his Chevy in her weedy drive.

I didn't know that he didn't even know that woman anymore or that that car had been sold down the river long before. He had taken another post with USAID, in Kabul, learned some Pashtu, moved in with his secretary, discarded his memories of Southeast Asia (the pet monkey, the state dinner where they served chicks baked in egg cups, the impotent .22 he hid in a nightstand drawer, his wife and newborn son) and replaced them with Khan and his tribes. My father, not one to keep photographs, worked, fucked, ate, and unsentimentally moved to Jakarta, Beirut, Paris.

Jesus Loves Me, This I Know, grape Kool-Aid and sandwich cookies, then the women helped me lift the Buddha onto the folding craft table like a baby at a baptism. "Oh, me," they said with rictus grins. The next kid showed off the crucifix his Daddy cut from sulfur coal, as black as sin and twice as oily.

I didn't know better than to draw on the Buddha, so it got buried for safekeeping in the trunk mysterious with camphor and cedar. For years I contemplated it from the outside. In my mind the trunk became something like the portmanteau Joan must have carried into battle, the carriage trunk Marie's footmen dropped to mutton stares, the kind of trunk Miss Havesham folded dowry into, Amanda Wingfield dragged up from the plantation, Amelia Earhart dragged down to the coral. The sort wheeled along platforms by Polish beauties as the Germans hit town. A trunk that someone like, oh, Margaret Bourke-White, Clare Boothe Luce, Pearl S. Buck, or Martha Gellhorn Hemingway skycapped on Pan Am when winging far away.

I didn't know why my mother became a recluse in the detritus of memory. Her humor seemed intact. When I released the dozens of cats held captive in our bathroom while we ate, they piled over each other coming out the door, claws and tails and terrified eyes, cascades of frantic cats suddenly freed like a river from a feline dam, and my mother laughed and laughed.

"Stampede!" she yelled, apparently delighted at the surreal anarchy of the world. Every spring they died of feline distemper, lay wrapped in newspaper like cold fish while we dug together in the side yard, furtive as grave robbers. Our shovels grated on previous years' delicate old bones.

I didn't know, but my mother told me, that she had always done what she liked, laughed how she got a pilot's license in secret when Daddy wouldn't let her enlist, how he forced the annulment with that first man, but anyway she'd worked for *Life*, had a master's, taught in West Palm Beach, had two other husbands, and now threw rejected washing machine baskets high into railcars on the siding of a filthy factory at sixty-two years of age. There was something funny in that I didn't know.

When we took her from her house and put her in a home, she smirked and nodded with palsy. Mute and demure. I knew it all along, she seemed to imply. Cleaned out the debris, piles of old news, cat-pissed divan, lamps cancered with rust, ruined beds clothes sacks piano pots and that trunk, which I broke open with a knife, the key long gone, to find the Eternal within. It rests now, for a mote in its geologic mind, on my shelf in the sun.

I didn't know until I was thirty-three and my mother's brain had gone smooth that it's not the Buddha at all but smiling Quan Am, she "who-listens-to-the-world's-cries," bodhisattva of compassion for those who suffer, because they remember, because pain is supremely democratic, because they hold back to pass on bitter wisdom; for those who, afraid of impermanence, need something cold and heavy to hold, to hoard, to treasure, to lie inside, to prove they're still alive.

What did I know about

a woman

smiling?

The Unknown

I was glazing the Christmas ham when my elder son's shrieks of delight, audible over the storm and stress of a busy kitchen, set my parental senses tingling. Out in the living room I found Starbuck in his Buzz Lightyear suit, wings, spats, and flashlight glasses, flying over the heads of our guests in the arms of his uncle Richard. There were a couple of things my brother-in-law didn't know.

Starbuck spent forty hours a week at an expensive Montessori school poring over superhero taxonomy with his pals. (Is there really a Super Fantastic Strong Man?) He had come home the first day and said it was agreed: David was Superman, Inhoo was Spider-Man, and he was Batman. In a way, I was proud. Superman is so obvious, with his square jaw and puritan rectitude, like Ronald Reagan with a spit curl. Spider-Man is OK but just a kid. Given the choice, I'd be Batman, too. At least he worked for his powers. But I wasn't sure I wanted our three-year-old emulating an angst-ridden, middle-aged angry guy in latex who calls himself the Dark Knight.

Blame it on my upbringing. My mother never capitulated on pop-culture violence. For comics I had Scrooge McDuck, and my sister's Baby Hueys. (My mother didn't mind *Mad* magazine, mind you; she was a nonviolent subversive.) Our television broke when I was four and was never fixed, so I dropped out of the TV zeitgeist at *Daktari* (which co-starred a cross-eyed lion named Clarence) and didn't return until the fifth season of *Magnum, P.I.*—a gap of some twenty years.

Sure, when other grade-school kids, avid as *New Yorker* critics, parsed the performance of Andre the Giant as Big Foot in *The Six Million Dollar Man*, I suffered. Then I went home and cataloged all my books by the Dewey decimal system (*William H. McGuffey: Boy Reading Genius*, j.921/MCG). And I'm okay.

Still, I thought, maybe Starbuck would benefit from leniency. If we let him hide under the dinner table and gobble Pez from his Batman dispenser, he might become one of those superhumanly cool kids who succeed at everything. He'd be a running back and class president; he'd snowboard Whistler and start a band; every summer he'd build houses with Habitat. Eventually, he'd practice medicine with Doctors Without Borders, where he'd meet a beautiful daughter of France, and together they'd run a clinic and raise their own babies in Paris while he wrote his trilogy on the human comedy, in which there would figure largely a beneficent, wise father.

Before I could enjoy all that, I had to face the first tenet of superheroes, their reason for being: to "poom" bad guys, as Starbuck said. (This was not to be confused with the infinitive "to boom": an intransitive verb. "The dog boomed" meant she slipped while running to the food bowl. "Poom" was a transitive verb requiring a direct object. Correct usage dictated: "Starbuck poomed the iPod with a plastic golf club until his father boomed to the floor in a fit of apoplexy.") We sat together and talked about cartoon pooming and real pooming, and how people get hurt, and how the only time we ever hit another person is in certain sports, such as one called boxing, which I don't really watch, because violence of any kind is antithetical . . .

"What's boxing, Daddy?" he asked guilelessly.

I try to reward curiosity, so I explained that certain athletes who train very hard to be strong and tough use their skills in carefully monitored sporting events called . . .

"What's training?" Starbuck asked.

I said boxers hit punching bags, but we don't have a bag or even a picture of one, so here, hit my palms, like this. He slapped at my hands with an overhand flail that promised to jam his wrists, so I showed him the mechanics of a jab and how to tuck in the thumb. He got the form but was hesitant, and since I want him to embrace physicality, I encouraged him to hit harder and then harder still. He grimaced and punched and grunted and punched.

"Harder!" I said. "Come on, *hit* me!"

Only after an hour or two, when he could really drive one in, did we stop to ice my hands.

My brother-in-law, who loves Starbuck as if he were his own son, knew none of these facts; they lay under the surface of happy times like a drowned tree waiting to rip open a riverboat. Richard simply saw that the boy was getting too excited and set him down, making the excuse that he, Uncle Zurg, needed to catch his breath before he destroyed this measly planet. That's when Starbuck, a.k.a. Buzz Lightyear—Defender of the Galaxy— poomed him in the testicles, as superheroes will.

~~~

I didn't know if I would get poomed by student work at the end of the semester. I had told creative-writing students not just to revise their stories but to re-envision them, and rhetoric students to shape twenty-page essays from messy, massive project notebooks and earlier drafts. Who knew what I'd get? I'd become so immersed in their projects that I felt trapped in them, blinded, as in a dream where you try to run in hobnail boots while some unseen evil, smelling of those shrimp you ate that sat out too long, chases you. Strangely, I also dreaded letting go and facing the sudden silence that comes at the end of every semester. But a number of stressors prevented that from happening.

One was the inevitable squawking over grades. A demure student with downcast eyes listened to my reasons for her participation grade (she never spoke in class, even when called on), then sprouted claws and fangs, and jumped at my throat. Another told me that a D in my course meant he'd have to join the Marines and would be in Iraq by Easter. (This is a variant of plea-demands by foreign students who tell me their government will recall them in public disgrace, possibly for dismemberment, if they don't get at least a B-plus from me. An A-minus would be more in line with Amnesty International guidelines.)

There was also—*mirabile dictu*—notification of a job interview for a tenure-track position at a good liberal-arts college, ranked somewhere between

Amherst College and Transylvania University by *U.S. News & World Report.*
I couldn't have boomed over any harder if I'd been poomed.

Of course, I've had many job interviews, including one, after I finished my bachelor's, that should have inoculated me against anything to come. The small-business owner—he called himself a CEO—twisted an onyx ring around his pinkie and used the time to talk about framed photos of himself with the town's mayor, later indicted for fraud. As I was leaving, he called me back and pressed a button on a keychain gadget his company sold as a sideline.

"Fuck you," it said in a robot voice.

I grinned uncertainly.

He pushed another button, and the thing said, "Eat shit." Then the man did the meanest thing anyone had ever done to me: he gave me the job.

But hiring for tenure-track English professors is different from anything else, including adjunct teacher hiring. Interviews are held at one of two professional conferences, the first being the Modern Language Association meeting, between Christmas and New Year's. Like most big conferences, it rotates among cities with expensive hotels, dining, shopping, and entertainment. That year, it was in Washington, D.C.

It's said that it takes money to make money, and this enterprise cost us several hundred dollars at the Men's Wearhouse and—since Mrs. Churm and Starbuck would go with me—the price of gas for the minivan in lieu of an airline ticket, three meals a day for three, enough coffee and Pringles to get me over the mountains, and a stay in the Embassy Suites in Georgetown.

The MLA conference has been mocked by the press as irrelevant and elitist. For me it was about the chance at a better-paying, secure job in my field, and seeing old friends. (One of the rarely discussed hazards of adjunctdom is the constant cycle of making and then losing friends as people are forced to move to other jobs. It wrecks community—I've seen nothing like it since the army—and it helps perpetuate the use of contingent labor.)

As it turned out, then, in the last two weeks of December I would need to: grade more than a thousand pages of student writing; tally final grades and report them; provide daycare for at least one of our sons, once Starbuck's school closed for the holidays; find a tree, put up a tree, decorate a tree;

document and justify my entire intellectual and creative being in a portfolio of materials for the hiring committee; design a yearlong symposium for first-year students (a requirement at the hiring college); find out what sorts of questions I might be asked in interview and drill myself on the answers; clean the house for guests; prepare the holiday meal; pretend not to be distracted for guests and mediate any pooming; shop for clothes; answer mail; arrange freelance work; plan and prepare spring classes; and participate in Christmas morning under the influence of several mimosas.

This left to Mrs. Churm only: her own job in the College of Education; gift shopping and mailing; bill paying; laundering; photography of the boys and subsequent Christmas-card writing and mailing; sick-cat ferrying to the vet; and planning the twelve-hour drive to the coast. It's hard to show in print what it sounded like in our house then, but it was something like this:

"Why do you always let the lotion drip from the nozzle when you LUBE YOURSELF UP *AFTER YOUR SHOWER* SO IT GETS ON STARBUCK'S BATH TOYS *AND NOW THERE'S* HAIR *STUCK ALL OVER THEM?!* "

The process of my interview, at least, didn't have to be an unknown. Hinterland's Department of English had a Method that explained the job search and they thought gave their grad students an advantage on the market. (If their grads were hired, the department looked effective. That attracted better new students, who were, in turn, more marketable, and so it goes.) But some felt that no one else, especially any Ivy League types who might be hiding in the shrubbery, should ever get their hands on The Method.

A couple of years earlier, the director of graduate studies (call him "the Little Scholar") had sent two e-mails to everyone in the department, announcing an open meeting: Come hear about The Method. At the time, I wasn't job-seeking, but The Method was for "interested faculty," too, so I went. Adjuncts were beginning to be let go, and the department had promised anything in its power to make the transition easier. But I'd forgotten that adjunct faculty weren't considered faculty, so this benefit would be withheld. (In one departmental meeting, a bony old woman stood and said, "Why don't you people go get real jobs?")

When the Little Scholar saw me—the product of another graduate program—watering down the eugenic stock of Hinterland's meeting, he asked me in front of everyone to leave. I didn't know the man and had liked his book on Faulkner, but when I met him in the library a week or two later, I leaned over him and said a couple of things. As my anger grew, I found myself quoting the Ed Harris loser character from *Glengarry Glen Ross*, which I'd been teaching: "What are you, friend to the working man, *Ricky*?" Needless to say, he didn't give me the printed pamphlet based on The Method, either.

~~~

We left for the MLA conference the morning after Christmas and drove through the day and into the night, through rain in the valleys and snow on the mountaintops, alongside the big trucks, around the long eastward bends graded the opposite way you'd expect, so it often felt like we were going over, which helped keep me awake. In back, Mrs. Churm slumped into her seat belt, her head on Starbuck's shoulder. Light from the DVD player flickered on the boy's exhausted face as he imprinted on his brain the basic rules for mysteries by playing the same five *Scooby-Doo* episodes in an endless loop. I hadn't even known there was a character named Scooby-Dumb, and it was a relief to emerge from the mad isolation of the highway into the lights of Wheeling. The city squatted on forested hills that rose from the cold river. Smoke poured from coal-fired plants.

"Starbuck, look," I said softly. "One of your great-grandfathers was in the coal mines, as a boy. An orphan. What a hard life. But he went on to be a union official and a politician."

Starbuck was obviously awed, because he stayed silent, thinking on it. A Scooby-Doo villain with the voice of Peter Lorre said, "Drats! You meddling kids."

"What would our ancestors have made of all this, Starbuck?" I said, waving at the detritus of fast food in our rolling living room, the high-speed road ahead, the unseen waiting luxury and artificial stress that deepened credit-card debt. "Don't you think it's odd how we move toward specific things but can't even name them? So much is unknown beforehand, it's a wonder we start journeys at all. Starbuck, are you listening to me?"

"Huh?" Starbuck said. He didn't know why grownups got so crazy-gone over nothing when there was a snow ghost that needed pooming.

Scooby-Doo giggled, "Eeheeheeheehee," in a descending scale, and I stuffed my mouth with potato chips. The boy had a lot to learn about quests and the dark hearts of fathers. We drove on, as families will.

Desire

I'm stretched out on my back on the desert floor. Aztecs torture my feet. I wake with a shout, and the two cats wrestling on the foot of our bed flee with their tails in the air. It's time to go.

〰

"There are more versions of desire in American culture than apocryphal Inuit words for snow," the scholar says. "Appetite, craving, hankering, hunger, itch, longing, lust, passion, pining, thirst, urge, yearning, yen. Compulsion, urge, zeal, liking, love, taste, eagerness, impatience, wish, want, need, avarice, cupidity, greed, rapacity. Are they really different things, or a matter of degrees?"

〰

We drive through West Virginia. I use the mountains to help me visualize the North Woods, where the hiring college is. We'll buy several acres and design a home to fit the site. It'll have the hammerbeam frame of a fifteenth-century barn, with clerestory windows along the ridgeline to flood the upper floor with light. I'll cross-country ski to work and have just one drink before dinner, and a lot of writing will get done, a lot of writing. It all sounds very Scott-Fitzgerald-at-Juan-les-Pins, but it's really true.

〰

We follow the parkway along the Potomac and cross Key Bridge. Mrs. Churm sinks into a swoon at the shops lining both sides of Georgetown's M Street. At a stoplight, I soak a tissue with cold Snapple and dab her temples. Signs for L'Occitane, Sephora, and Dean & Deluca flicker on the lenses of her glasses, as in some tragic movie about desire.

～～～

"I want the very best of everything."

—ERNEST HEMINGWAY

～～～

Starbuck won't sleep in the inflatable Spider-Man bed he insisted we bring from Inner Station, so his knees poke my back all night. For a while, I conduct a mock interview in my head, then I'm driving again, up a mountainside in West Virginia. When I look at the passenger seat, Starsky is riding shotgun. We approach the cloud-whipped summit along a crumbling shale ledge. I look over again; now Hutch is in the passenger seat. I wake and think: This is the examined life?

～～～

The conference is so big it commands three hotels. I'm interviewed by a very nice man who happens to be head of the English Department and by a very nice woman who happens to be a Benedictine sister as well as a professor of English. They explain that they need someone not only to teach but also to bring together a cooperative agreement with a very good literary press, a reading venue in a big city, and a visiting authors' series. The job is more than I thought. It's the sort of situation I thrive in. Damn it.

～～～

"You made me love you.
I didn't want to do it, I didn't want to do it . . .
You made me happy sometimes, you made me glad,
But there were times, dear, you made me feel so bad."

—JUDY GARLAND

"We'll let everyone know, either way, by January 7th," the interviewers say. I head for the Irish pub across from the Sheraton. It's a good place, except for the TV sets over the bar and the academics on every stool and chair.

"Why the devil do we portray the devil having so much fun?" a scholar at a table says. "Because he's pure id, desire without constraint, and that's *exactly* why we need him."

"Desire is a mental house of cards, a construction that can't bear the weight of reality," his colleague says. "Ask all those lost souls who got everything they imagined, and more. Where is your M. C. Hammer *now*?"

A lone academic at the bar drinks a single pint of Bass, gets a little tipsy, pays up. He stops under the awning out front and fumbles with his raincoat, as if it's new to him. The only other patron on the freezing patio is an older man with poet's hair, a florid face, and a two-toned lap dog. He says to the academic, in a nearly unintelligible brogue, "You're not leaving us already, then?" The academic grins and does a little streetwise head tilt at the man.

"You have to pet my doggy," the Irishman says.

"Do what now?" the academic says.

"You can't be leavin' without pettin' my little doggy." There's a hint of threat in the Irishman's voice. The academic strokes the man's sheltie as he's told.

I was the academic. Well dressed and half-lit (both to the limits of my budget), I walk on, drawing admiring stares from people on the street.

~~~

The interview went well, I tell Mrs. Churm. We're back in our suite. Starbuck jumps from couch to chair to floor to couch, Batman cape askew. "It went really well. I asked Sister Tara back here for pay-per-view and microwave popcorn."

"You didn't," Mrs. Churm says. "Did you?"

~~~

I'm eight. We're in the hotel at Our Lady of the Snows Shrine in Belleville, Illinois, not because we're Catholic, or far from home, but because my mother admires the Kennedys and Graham Greene. But she's not one for rules either. She dips her index finger in a wall font and playfully dabs holy water on my left cheek. One minute later, while she's in the bathroom, I misjudge my leap from bed to chair, smack my face, and begin to howl. Instant shiner, right where the holy water was.

"All the nuns are going to think I beat you," my mother says in the shrine restaurant.

~~~

"Would you like to talk about your dissertation?" Sister Tara asks.

I feel so at ease that I lean back, unbutton my jacket, and throw my arm across the back of their couch. For a millisecond, I wonder if the Benedictine obligation to hospitality is making me overconfident. Then I expound. "In my diss I investigate tropes of female strength in the poetry of Hunter Davis. Do you know his late work 'Just Like Mom'?"

I recite the poem:

Mary Ann Barnes is the queen of all the acrobats,
She can do the things that'll give a guy the fits,
She can shoot green peas from her fundamental orifice,
Do a triple somersault and catch 'em on her tits.
She's a great big son-of-a-bitch, twice the size of me.
Got hair on her ass like branches on a tree!
She can shoot, fight, fuck, fly a plane and drive a truck.
She's the kind o' girl who's gonna marry me.

The two professors look at each other and nod almost imperceptibly. I think: I'm doing it!

The scholar sips at a whiskey-and-water and grimaces. His gastric reflux is pretty bad. "We portray Satan smirking, living it up, because we want to punish ourselves for the fun we'd like to have. We absolutely want what he's got to sell, but believe that the consequences of desire must be suffering."

We're in the hotel lobby, on the way to lunch with friends. A cab is waiting, and Starbuck can't get the Pez into his Batman dispenser. He refuses to budge and sobs as if his heart is broken. People stare at the boy's bad parents.

"Tell us about your dissertation," the department head says.

"Scooby-Doo is a narratological paradigm for the shift of all cultural artifacts from integrity to fragmentation," I say. "The episode 'That's Snow Ghost' emulates a kind of realist tradition, the mirror traveling down the road. Then Bakhtin's 'polyphony' emerges with the addition of a chorus—Scooby-Dumb, Scrappy-Doo—who voice things the culture wishes to say but can't due to the formal strictures of Scooby's personality and his doggy speech impediment. Inevitably, self-reflexive commentary on the show's own processes comes with the shift to the postmodern, as when Fred is forced to ride in the back of the van for the first time in decades and says in surprise, 'So this is what it's like to ride back here.' Finally, a feminist Daphne emerges, as in 'Scooby-Doo on Zombie Island,' concurrently with the literalization of the supernatural—the zombies are real now, not criminals in zombie suits, and they thank the gang for solving the mystery and releasing their souls into 'peace.' The text has exhausted itself, even assured its own destruction."

The interviewers beam. "You're doing it!" they exclaim.

"You made me love you.

You made me love you, babe, made me love you, babe,

Made me love you, babe (oh Lord), made me love you, babe . . .

Made me love you, babe (said it wasn't in my plans), made me love you, babe.

Ooh, look at you."

—R. KELLY

〜〜

I'm ten. I lust for the half-size Model A replica with the lawnmower engine in the florist's showroom, to be given away in a drawing. It's just as the Buddha said. Later, of course, there are many desires, which I try to knock out, like patches of infant eczema treated with steroidal cream. But in the presence of some new temptation, desire comes raging back. This interview wakes a lust in me for things I never knew I wanted—the entire Penguin Classics library, an Egyptian dhow to sail on a nearby river, a pet Compsognathus I could walk on a leash. They're all dreams of repose, punctuated with adventure.

〜〜

Interview over, I attend a panel session on humor. One scholar has flown in all the way from Hong Kong to talk about a parody of a joke she's identified in her research.

"I call my paper 'The Territorial Shaggy Dog,'" she says. "It focuses on the redundantly no-point shaggy-dog shaggy-dog [*sic*] story."

Another speaker says humor studies is "pretty serious," and calls his paper, "What Is This, a Joke?" He explains the transmission of jokes through society and tells one himself:

"What's the difference between President Clinton and the *Titanic*? We know how many people went down on the *Titanic*."

The audience is appreciative.

~~~

"Too bad we won't see you this trip," I tell Frenchy on the phone. "Free drinks every night in the courtyard, and we've got a pullout couch." Two hours later he calls to say he's most of the way to D.C.

At happy hour, Starbuck squeezes behind him on the settee. "You've got a baldie head," he says, massaging it, then eats fourteen maraschino cherries and runs through the crowd around the popcorn machine in his Batman cape. Our German friend, also here for the conference, joins us. Frenchy recalls childhood trips to the Black Forest and sings to her: "*Schön ist die Welt, drum Brüder, lasst uns reisen wohl in die weite Welt, wohl in die weite Welt. . . .*"

~~~

Just before my interview, I sit in the Sheraton lobby, memorizing pedagogic goals for composition classes. I glance up. My nemesis from Hinterland, the Little Scholar, who blocked me from obtaining job-hunting help, approaches. We nod.

"No suffering laid upon us by nature or chance or fate is so painful as that inflicted by the will of another," I say. "Schopenhauer."

He replies: "How's that adjunct thing working out for you?"

~~~

Frenchy and I walk to a Vietnamese restaurant. He tells me about his great-grandfather, a French artist who decorated hotels in the American South. His son wanted nothing to do with the business and went back to France after World War I to pass off coupons out of cereal boxes as American money. Frenchy's dad worked for the great-grandfather and remembered him standing on a ladder, painting roses on ballroom ceilings, all day long.

~~~

Disorientation of sleeplessness and stress. I've played too many mental games with myself, like a method actor tuning his mood. I look at the dark highway but fantasize about Minnesota, remember Washington, and anticipate Inner Station. I think of how long it once took to travel from the coast to the Mississippi, and how this cold rain smells like Scotland's. It's a long ride. In our driveway I open the sliding door on the van. Happy Meal toys spill down like sand in an hourglass. The house is Holiday Inn—not Kimpton—clean, but it's good to be home. I've never been so hungry.

~~~

"Mar-arge, I'aave been watching women's volleyball on ESPN...."
   —HOMER SIMPSON

~~~

January 7 comes and goes, as do the ninth, twelfth, sixteenth. Rationalizations begin: They're getting special permission from the provost to skip the campus interviews and hire me directly. They're keeping me on the hook in case the person they offered the job declines. I lie sweating into the sheets. At the door to the bedroom, my writing stands silently in the darkness, accusing.

~~~

Homer Simpson scrubs himself in the shower. "Must ... wash off ... stink of failure," he says through gritted teeth.

~~~

But I'm hired. I take a couple of days and drive up to the Catholic women's college to organize my new office. A student welcoming committee comes around as I'm putting books on the shelves. A vivacious sophomore says, "Every Tuesday we have a D. H. Lawrence reading group around the fire pit and roast weenies and ooey-gooey marshmallows, Professor Churm. Will you be my blanket buddy?"

"Young lady, that's not funny," I say sternly.

~~~

Frenchy drinks another Bia Saigon. "We were in Plei Djerang, and Johnny and his buddy were jostlin' each other and kiddin' each other and givin' each other a little shove here and there. Johnny was sharpenin' his survival knife, and his buddy said something funny to him, and Johnny kinda grinned at him and stuck that knife out at him, and 'course he was a little bit drunk and his depth perception was a little off, so he drove that knife into his buddy about a quarter-inch. His buddy yelled, 'Damn, Johnny, you stuck me!' Johnny said, 'Well, hell, I pulled it right back out.'"

〰️

Starbuck and I wait for Mrs. Churm in the Inner Station mall. He spots an arcade claw game and wants me to try for the little stuffed Pluto dog inside. I have only three dollars on me. We try, fail. Try again, fail. All this recent *wanting* has left me feeling that if my little boy doesn't get that cartoon dog. . . . Last try, the hooks catch in its scarf and it drops down the chute. Starbuck is delighted. I'm shaky and exhausted.

〰️

It's a Thursday. Baby Wolfie sits up for the first time and says, "'Hope is the confusion of the desire for a thing with its probability.' Schopenhauer. Now, as long as I have the power of speech, may I take this opportunity to say . . . ah, what the hell, there's time." He sticks the cat's tail in his mouth and gums it.

〰️

I reach for Mrs. Churm, and she reaches back. We fall backward together thirteen years and land with a thump in a 1986 Toyota Corolla parked in an empty lot outside the Rainforest Café in Schaumburg, Illinois.

〰️

"I want to say that you were one of our top 14 candidates out of 165 applications. However, in that pile of applications, we had editors of major journals; we had people with many novels or volumes of poetry published; we had at least 100 applications from people who had PhDs as well as MFA degrees and multiple publications from houses such as Norton; in short, the competition for this position was pretty strong."

—ENGLISH DEPARTMENT HEAD OF THE HIRING COLLEGE

"... he asked me would I yes to say yes my mountain flower and first I put my arms around him yes and drew him down to me so he could feel my breasts all perfume yes and his heart was going like mad and yes I said yes I will Yes."
—JAMES JOYCE

Etc.

Confessions

Let's say you're lucky enough to know an actual California hippie poet with a bushy ponytail and Tijuana retread sandals, the kind of guy who made it to forty without a credit card. He's a moralist who wrote a poem about the exploitation of dwarf miners and a sensualist who calls you his father-confessor. (If he calls you his mother-confessor, tighten your belt.)

Back in the day, you guzzled beer while he confessed his sins, which he made interesting and funny. (Even priests must appreciate that.) First, he confessed to sleeping with your teaching mentor. Weeks later, he lay with a woman who was in love with your gay South African friend. Sometime after that, the poet regretted a fling with a visiting assistant professor, who turned out to be so . . . emotional. As he talked on those humid afternoons, squirrels with nearly hairless tails shuffled in the fallen palm fronds, and grackles stole french fries from his plate. Once, he confessed to eating nightshade flowers in somebody's yard and passing out in an unlocked car on the street. Oh, one last thing—he'd forgotten his wallet; would you mind picking up the tab, this once?

Confessions made to clergy are like those canisters at the bank drive-through: they chuff up the pneumatic pipe to God, who waits for eternity to cash the penitent's check. But secular confessions are more like caltrops, which look like toy jacks but have razor edges and one sharp point always sticking up. They're bloody little forget-me-nots: I enjoy this, they say; remember that about me and worry a little; I have witnessed something disturbing, and I may go back for more; think of me thus and so, as I believe myself to be.

The person who confesses fits Tolstoy's definition of an artist, who "hands on to others feelings he has lived through. . . . Others are infected by these feelings and also experience them." In this way, confessions, like art, provide a little immortality.

One day, watching the *Beverly Hillbillies* episode where they go to England and Jethro starts calling himself Sir Jethro de Bodine, head varlet to the Earl of Clampett, you roll over, and somebody's old confession, hidden in the pocket of the jacket you were wearing when it was offered, pricks like conscience. Have you thought of the poet lately?

It's been seven years, you remember—no, closer to eight now—since he blew into town after a poetry retreat in the Ouachitas. He was hours late getting to the house, but you found him a ham and three or four side dishes, a cherry pie with whipped cream, and a pitcher of sweet tea, for a midnight snack. Then he sipped delicately at a twelve-pack and settled in to talk. You had an infant who would wake at 1:30 in the morning and again at 3:00, 4:30, and 6:00, but the poet was so full of good humor that when he said he couldn't stay more than a week or two, you felt strong mixed emotions. You put him in the spare bedroom, with the cats' litter box. After a light breakfast of a dozen eggs over easy, hash browns, a pound of bacon, and homemade biscuits and gravy, he spent several hours out in the yard on a cell phone. But he loved the Inner Station Fourth of July parade, doubling with laughter at the float bearing the banner, "We'd do ANYTHING for our country," and you were reminded of his fine moral sense.

His last confession was that he was moving from Pennsylvania, where he was an adjunct, back to south Florida, with an older woman who was a waitress and her kids. The memory of how you thought it was wrong that he slept past noon, and of him stretching luxuriously under the comforter to the sound of a cat fervently clawing in its box, makes you feel guilty and worried all over again.

Al Pacino, as real-estate shill Ricky Roma in the film version of *Glengarry Glen Ross*, says, "All train compartments smell vaguely of shit. It gets so you don't mind it. That's the worst thing that I can confess. You know how long it took me to get there? A long time."

Roma might have confessed worse; at the time, he's seducing a lonely man into buying swampland. But I know what he means. The Monday stink of stale beer and garbage outside a campus bar reminds me of a Panamanian brothel where we used to drink because it was cheap and the jukebox played "One Night in Bangkok." La Guardia stood near the bar, under a velvet painting not unlike Manet's *Olympia*, with their Uzis pointed at their feet, and the urinal troughs were filled with lemons and limes. Outside, a boy grilled some kind of sweetish meat over a charcoal brazier.

"Hey, Jimmy Dean pork sausage!" he yelled.

"That ain't no Jimmy Dean," we always said, and we always bought several of the kebobs and ate hungrily.

Like other stories we tell, confessions show how we choose to think of our lives and what we like to focus on. They even hint at how we would fashion heaven, given the chance. Problem is, some people's ideas of heaven are commonly known as hell. As Ricky Roma says, "Bad people go to hell? I don't think so. If you think that, act that way. A hell exists on earth? Yes. I won't live in it. That's me."

And so, while we care about our families, friends, and students, their enthusiasms can grow tiresome. (Mrs. Churm returned from a conference and said eight times in two hours that she attended the "opening plenary session." I hung myself with my belt.)

Evangelicals from Colorado often invaded Hinterland. The ringers huddled together in their cowboy hats in prayer circles on the quad. Wind gusts reached forty miles per hour, but they gamely held aloft flags clumsily sewn from bedsheets, which read, "All That Matters Is You Are All Headed for Hell."

One day two matriculated jokers stood nearby with cardboard signs on which they'd scrawled, "You are fine" and "Free hugs." One smirked at me and said, "Everything's going to be OK." I thanked him for that, and he looked surprised.

~~~

Many of my undergrads at Hinterland carried twenty-hour course loads in subjects like genetic engineering and *also* worked thirty hours in that basement laboratory with all the hazmat placards. In office-hour confessionals, they told me, unprompted, other reasons they were doing poorly in my class: Dad killed Mom, and the trial was that week. I'm not making that up or being flip; how do students survive this? Maybe one can memorize Planck's constant under these circumstances, but what of the Confessional Poets? As Ovid says, "Nothing that is hard can a sick mind endure." (When I get physically sick, I can't read literature. It's the worst thing I can confess. You know how long it took me to get there? A long time.)

But I'm not talking about disasters as unavoidable as fate. I'm talking about drama—how we use our imaginations and free will to shape our lives. I'm talking about Jerry, my independent-study kid, who found it fascinating that he couldn't get himself to our meetings and said we needed to discuss not only his novel draft but also what made him do self-defeating things. Or the student nearly my age who confessed, in harrowing after-class sessions, her abuse by her husband, yet smiled grimly all the while. Uncomfortable and uncertain, I mentioned resources available to her.

"Yes, I know," she said. "It's just that he's keeping me from what I want. . . ."

The talk—and her martyred laughter—continued, until she looked beatific. Six months later I saw her in a video store, and she introduced her husband, who crushed my hand and glowered. She seemed excited that I knew of him and that I could see she was pregnant.

Henry James knew that if people believe they suffer, they do. It's good news for Henry James, who can then focus his stories on psychological nuance instead of on big actions, like, say, Bruce Willis running across broken glass in his bare feet.

~~~

The air turned wet and cold; trees were mostly stripped of leaves. I parked by the graveyard at the edge of campus and, in a rush to get to the library myself, felt ill at the intent, tired, angry student faces I met on the street. I sometimes worried they weren't, as Wendell Berry says, "set free from fashionable lies"—other people's insistence on what's important. Jackhammers chattered, and a cherry picker crept through the crowds, carrying drywall for another new building in the College of Business.

Blood thumped in my ears as I climbed three flights of stone steps in the library. It smelled of dust and dry rot in the hallway where old card catalogs sat abandoned. High above them on the wall were fire alarms that looked as if they were salvaged from a Soviet submarine. If they worked at all, they wouldn't klaxon. "Oh, what's the use?" they'd sigh. Somewhere a librarian shouted, "Next!" Her tone was not encouraging.

Still, the reference room was my favorite place to work on campus. It was three hundred feet long and could seat five hundred, though there were never more than six or eight people around after they moved the reference desk to a more central location. The sun shone through gigantic fan windows with panels of stained glass set in them like jewels. Comfortable oak armchairs were tucked under endless oak tables; each table had a dictionary stand with an edition of *Webster's* in which the name "Harry Truman" had yet to be entered. Fumed oak shelves around the walls held sixteen thousand largely unused reference books, such as *The Complete Holdings of the Bancroft Library*, in thirty-nine volumes. Sitting under the high coffered ceilings and acanthus-leaf friezes, I imagined it as my own British Museum reading room, but a librarian friend told me it was to be renovated to make better use of the space.

~~~

I was thinking of false connections: autumn is the fall, and The Fall refers to Original Sin. It's a season for reflection and melancholy, what with the impending death of the earth and all, and a fine time for confessions. But the squirrels in my neighborhood didn't know jack about all that. They were so jazzed they couldn't stop chattering and tumbling high in the branches, scolding me and chasing each other in spirals up and down the trunks. One lost its grip and fell thirty feet to the ground, landing with an audible "oof" at the feet of Leo Tolstoy, our black Lab mix. The Count was so surprised he just stood there and looked at it. The squirrel tore off and in the next hour shucked the magnolia of its buds, dug up my crocuses, and started gnawing his way into the gable of the house. He and his buddies were content in their acorn fat and impudent hair, bucktoothed-ignorant of our notions of how life is meant to go.

Our two little boys, more and more like Thing One and Thing Two from *Cat in the Hat* ("They will give you some fun / On this wet, wet, wet day"), were warm and happy too. Mrs. Churm struggled to write code for her short-lived eBay business, and Thing One, waving a handful of neon Play-Doh, asked, "Mommy, do you want a meatball chocolate ice-cream cake with corn on it?" She referred the boy to me.

But to me he said, "Um, Daddy? I have a thing in my pocket that defeats things. It's probably T. Rex's. It's a super-duper trumpet laser. Here, Daddy. Here. Here, Daddy. Parasaurolophus is the one to drive now. Hey, put your seatbelt on."

It was hard to know what to say to this, other than, "Clearly, Son, you'll be a Harvard man."

I sat on the couch with a cup of tea, six books at various stages of being read, another 100 pages of student writing to grade before I could sleep, and all sorts of half-baked holiday plans, starting with Thanksgiving dinner for sixteen. I still needed to buy something that sounded like harness bells, since we had a secret room (honestly) behind the fireplace, and in a month I intended to hide there and shout "Ho! Ho! Ho!" and jingle the hell out of those bells, while three-year-old Thing One shivered in his bed with terror and delight.

Suddenly, a possum screamed in the backyard, and Mrs. Churm yelled, "Where's the dog?" The house emitted some damp confession from a cavity in its brick walls, and the stench of asparagus cooked in 1871 drifted past. Little Thing Two squirmed and grinned up at me, all gums, and filled his diaper with a blast like Gabriel's trumpet.

Whoever thought heaven had to be perfect? I just wished it could last.

Time Monkeys

Back in the twentieth century I was a catalog writer for one of America's biggest office-supplies companies. The work was easy, the pay adequate, the offices huge and bright. The cafeteria was subsidized, and I spent entire days there drinking coffee and reading literature instead of composing ads at my desk upstairs. In short, everything was great, and I disliked Plume Corp. the way you'd dislike drinking a big cup of warm spit.

There were signs that others felt the same. My boss, who looked exactly like smilin' Joe Garagiola, sat down one day to tell me a funny story. An elderly neighbor had given him a pair of beautiful spindle-backed chairs, and he'd taken them apart to refinish them. He laughed as he described replacing two back spindles in their holes while six others popped loose. He chuckled when he said he'd had to have a drink to calm down.

His face swelled as he told of returning to the wooden spindles waggling like evil fingers, and of having no control over events in his life: the chairs thwarted him, as did his former business partner, his ex-wife, his kids, his dog, and everyone in the Plume head office. He spoke so long that the earth tilted away from the sun, and winter came. When he finally found his way back to the punch line, he admitted he drank six more double gins and smashed the old woman's chairs to flinders with a maul.

Crazy Larry worked at Plume then too and invented time monkeys to explain the anguish of the place, how someone could sit down to chat and you'd suffer months of bitterness in a single afternoon. Larry said the monkeys are smiling and fanged. They wear fezzes. They chatter incessantly and pick at your clothes, creating all sorts of distractions and distortions: good times become brief, and dental work eternal. Essentially, they work against hope. If you think you're going to "just get through today" and then the rest of the week will be fine, if you're sure that your $1,000-a-head weekend at Club Med will feel like summers did when you were a school-child, rest assured: the monkeys are on their way.

~~~

Another fall semester began, marking my anniversary as a columnist with *McSweeney's*. To celebrate, *McSweeney's* and I renewed our vows in a quiet ceremony in Malibu, then flew to Saint-Tropez. You know how those forced milestones go. I wanted a salad; *McSweeney's* ordered the duck. I said we should drive over to Johnny Depp's and surprise him; *McSweeney's* insisted we find a phone and call first. By the time we flew home, *McSweeney's* had started smoking again and was giving me those looks like, *You got something you want to say to me? Because you look like you're feeling froggy. If you're feeling* froggy, *go ahead and* jump.

~~~

The process of writing about something—even your own life—breaks up and re-forms your sense of it. Rereading my writing disorients me, especially since I've never been a lecturer at a big state university at all; I'm a head in a jar on a shelf in the *McSweeney's* basement. I know rationally that what I perceive as the world is just editor John Warner showing film strips to all us heads, but when fellow columnist Roy Kesey's head, in the jar next to mine, mutters in its sleep about mad pursuits and wild ecstasies, I long for the imagined life I've written, like some amniotic Pinocchio.

~~~

We all fall victim to time's monkeyshines, once we're old enough to have compartmented pasts. The faces in my memory now include those of child-hood and hometown, other towns and cities, family, army, various schools, friendships, relationships, and workplaces, including the two thousand or so students I've taught at three universities. I'll sometimes see people I know across the quad, but reason puts them down, one by one, explaining to me that *that* person would have graduated years ago; that *other* person lived in Oxnard, California, and likely would have no reason to be here; I'd better *hope* that third one isn't who I think it is, or there'll be trouble.

"Betty?" I called. I was walking near the union when I spotted her. Betty and I were in Mrs. Scherer's seventh-grade English class and memorized all the prepositions together. It's odd she was in Inner Station and that she looked as she did in the late 1980s, when I last saw her, but maybe she became a university employee like me, and maybe she did Pilates.

"Excuse me. Betty Cooper, is that you? It's me, Oronte Churm."

The time monkeys obscuring her face shrieked and scattered.

The Kappa Delta glared. "Eww, Veronica," she said into her phone. "Did you hear that? This old guy's, like, totally *hitting* on me."

I seemed to be running afoul of time a lot. I watched my boys playing one evening and suddenly recalled my old G.I. Joe. My faded youth saddened me, and I wanted my toy back. Then I remembered other stuff. Joe was really just a piebald Ken doll handed down by my sister, and he stank of vinyl. He came with only a bathing suit, so I had to order his war kit from the back of a comic book. The pieces didn't match his scale, so his new helmet sat on the very top of his head like a tiny bowler hat. After a cousin sewed him a shapeless uniform, he looked like a Liberation Front guerrilla in gabardine. The poor bastard's final indignity, assuming he wasn't incinerated, is that he's still out there, smothered in a garbage dump, and won't decompose for five hundred years.

～～

A week before classes began, Mrs. Churm and I boarded a jet for south Florida with two little boys and high hopes for our rejuvenation. Time monkeys sipped champagne in first class and watched us trudge through to coach.

On the beach at Estero, the wrack of culture was washed ashore like sea glass. Here were our collective memories of the sea, all the wisdom of the watery parts of the world, from the Phoenicians onward: sailors' knots and pirates without menace and Junkanoo and anchors and talking seagulls, all painted on signs sprouting crazily, everywhere, shilling motels, nail salons, a Hooters, McDonald's, taverns, mopeds, ice cream, souvenirs, and Christ. Sweaty muscled people slapped volleyballs under a blazing sun then tucked into lasagne ai quattro formaggi and Oreo ice cream pie smothered with hot fudge at the Pastabilities & More.

Not to get all Hieronymus Bosch about this, but in the same picture there were anhingas standing crucified in the drainage canals, holding open their big wings to dry. At the goofy golf retention pond, alligators piled up promiscuously to beg for dog chow in Dixie cups. A white heron stood its turn with the suvs in the Wendy's drive-through, while sea crows scrabbled around on the vehicles' hoods and gobbled broken grasshoppers caught in wiper blades.

I felt a little sick at the jumble, and the 108-degree temperatures didn't help. But the time monkeys warned, *Settle in and enjoy the moment, or we'll strip it away.* Despite this, Starbuck refused to stick so much as a toe in the bathtub sea. Wolfie abandoned naps and crabbed through meals in expensive restaurants.

The spell was broken, as so often happens, in some dive. On San Carlos Island, shrimp trawlers dock behind the Beach Seafood Market and dump their hauls into the processing warehouse, where there's also a tiny retail shop and eight dining tables with views into the shrimp grading room. The restaurant is decorated with cases of Bud Light and wrinkled posters of fish and whales from *The Scandinavian Fishing Year Book*. Anti-slip mats lie on the concrete floor, which is channeled to drain fish drip: red snapper, grouper, and hogfish lie shiny-eyed in beds of crushed ice, and live blue crabs are stupid with cold to their fate. The smell hovers at the limits of tolerable authenticity, but we gratefully ate fresh fried shrimp, handmade hush puppies, and coleslaw, and drank sweet southern tea still warm around its ice cubes.

The next morning the heat had broken, and the wind smelled like damp white sand and the Gulf of Mexico, more Panhandle than 'Glades. Mottled slugs and seaweed lay at the high-water line, and schools of pilchards curved and leaped while we waded. Big ancient-looking snook, drawn dangerously close to shore to eat the shiners, may never have seen the pelicans fold and fall.

Up to the minute we had to leave, Starbuck shaped a castle with the fierce determination of a four-year-old, while one-year-old Wolfie gleefully clawed it down—two old gods at the timeless work of the world.

〜〜

We flew home. Another semester began with no way to predict its true duration. Another job season approached, and Mrs. Churm e-mailed me listings for nonteaching positions. Many things seemed possible, but the future was an unknown country, and there's no distance so great as time.

Quid Pro Quo, Dr. Lecter

Starbuck had been trying on new emotions, pretending he was mad or upset or joyous, then believing his invented states.

"You can't have any juice right now," Mrs. Churm told him. "You've had juice already. Have some water instead."

"You mean I can NEVER have juice again, never *ever* in a million trillion ducal-blaster years?" he wailed, practicing being hyperbolic.

He was especially fragile at dinnertime, even though he'd had a good day at school. He incited riots with his brother, then got upset when we said he was in trouble because he knew Wolfie copied everything he did.

"What am I going to have to do to get this pasta in you today?" I asked them tiredly, like a used-car salesman.

Starbuck ended up getting himself sent to his room before bedtime. Mrs. Churm went to say goodnight and said she expected better from him the next day. Starbuck looked past her at me as she lectured, and I shot him a look that was 60 percent, "You're gonna get it from me when your mother's done," and 40 percent, "You're gonna get wrestled down and kissed on the neck." His eyebrows went up hopefully.

I made him wait to find out which it would be until Mrs. Churm helped the boys say goodnight to each other and led Wolfie out of the room and down the hall. Starbuck tried to force the issue—"What? What are you going to do?" he pleaded, pretending terror—but I only looked sideways from the departing Mrs. Churm to Starbuck sitting on his pillow.

"Okay. Now," I said. I paused. "It's time you met . . . the Tickle Spider!"

My right hand ran toward him on its fingers, and he shrieked in delight. He sledge-hammered the spider with the bottom of his fist as it ran up his leg toward his armpits. He pulled it off him and sat on it, giggling, but intent and fierce. I let him struggle with it a minute, then said, "Wait, wait. Stop. Stop it."

"Huh?" he said. He stopped but wasn't about to get off the spider. Who would?

"Tickle Spider has something he wants to say," I said.

Starbuck shifted his weight off my hand—cautiously, cautiously—and held the spider down with both hands. He leaned down.

"What is it, Tickle Spider?" he asked.

"I want to tell you a secret," I whispered. "Come closer." Starbuck did. I said, "I want to tell you . . . I have . . . a *brother!*" With that, my other hand ran at him. Starbuck jerked back, allowing both Tickle Spiders to come at him at once. He screamed and began to sob.

I cradled him to my chest, said I was sorry, and reassured him. I felt horrible but pressed my lips together to keep from smiling. He made me promise never to bring out the Tickle Spider ever again, and I promised I never would, not in a million billion ducal-blaster years. I lay next to him as he calmed down, and just before he fell asleep, he asked the Tickle Spider to come and sleep on his chest.

~~~

I'd been promising Starbuck his first camping trip, Wolfie being still too young, and their godfather was visiting his own folks in our hometown, so I decided it was a good time for just the two of us to hit the road. Due to intangible fears (lions, tigers, and bears not being available in southern Illinois), camping in a tent somehow became sleeping in the back of our minivan. But that would mean buying mosquito netting for the windows, and in the end I reserved a "rustic cabin" at Giant City State Park, south of Carbondale. It's a lovely park I've visited since I was a boy, with a lodge built by the Civilian Conservation Corps from rough-hewn local timber and chiseled fieldstones.

The lodge always had a couple of original cabins nearby and a restaurant with excellent chicken dinners, but recently it had been sensitively updated with a bar, a swimming pool, and Wi-Fi. New cabins came in several sizes, from modest to Aspen townhouse, and the rustic cabin we chose had been totally rebuilt. Though plain, it had two comfortable full beds, a state-of-the-art shower room, and air-conditioning. We climbed to the observation deck on the water tower to look out over the hazy rolling hills toward the Mississippi and saw some early stars come out as the sun set.

Starbuck wanted ghost stories before bed. I was reluctant to get pulled into his new game of emotional bait-and-switch but told a watered-down version about a daddy and a boy camping in the woods. In the story, someone knocked on the door of their cabin (I used my foot to knock obviously on our door), and the monster turned out to be, mistakenly, the boy's godfather, carrying the Styrofoam box of leftover pizza they forgot at the restaurant where they'd just eaten dinner with the family.

It was a rotten story, and Starbuck spun his own gory tale, in which I had to play the part of the monster. When he vanquished me by pretending to spear my guts, I died obligingly and stuck my tongue out to the side, just a little. Then I very gently came back to life.

"Rarghh," I said, in the voice you'd say, "Cream and sugar, please."

Starbuck screamed and did the terror jig. He demanded tearfully that I sleep in his bed that night and wanted assurances that nothing could come in the door or windows.

I lay awake in the dark next to him. It was too early for my sleep. The air-conditioner was inefficient and roared each time it came to life, drowning out the cicadas and frogs, but it was too hot and humid outside to leave everything open. I thought I heard the bass line and barely intelligible words of a car stereo under the roar of the unit, but when the air cycled off, there was no music or car or words, only the Devonian woods.

Coolant gurgled in the pipes as the air-conditioner cleared its throat to start up again. A couple in the next cabin murmured in the night. I remembered there was no one in the next cabin. I thought about how the closet with the hot-water heater and the air unit were between us and the door. If the thing blew up or caught fire, we'd be trapped. Then it started up again, and I heard mutterings under the whistle and roar of its blower. I lifted my head a little from the pillow. We really were in the woods, after all, far from the nearest town and any help. In fact, there was almost no one in the 4,000-acre park, since it was the middle of the week. I lay there listening to the monster in the closet and all the noises under its racket—the chuckling, the salivations of the beast, the scrape of a convict's shoe on concrete somewhere nearby, and the rasp of the file he was using to free himself from ball and chain.

It was a long night, and wonderful.

Show, Don't Tell

"The soul has no assignments," Randall Jarrell says. "It wastes its time."
That's never more obvious than when you're trying to teach your five-year-
old everything he needs to know about the place you grew up so that he'll
become, well, *you*.

"Thank you, Daddy, for teaching me all these things," he says politely,
trapped in his car seat by a five-point harness. "But, Daddy? Can we get
hamburgers for lunch or not?"

Most know little about southern Illinois. It's at the same latitude as
Richmond, Virginia, and had a strong secessionist movement, despite
Grant using Cairo to control the Mississippi and Ohio Rivers. (My father
remembered an anvil on display in the town where he grew up that had
been broken, in one of the town's anniversary celebrations of Lincoln's murder, by "shooting" it—loading gunpowder into it and blowing it sky-high.
One wishes fewer had dodged it on its way back down.) The voices sound
mid-southern, especially those of older people, who've distilled local speech
with age.

Southern Illinoisans eat according to various cultures that worked the
mines—grits, biscuits and gravy, ham steaks with gravy, fried chicken with
mashed potatoes and gravy, black-eyed peas, greens, and God's own sweet
corn and tomatoes; costolette, scaloppini, rolladi, lasagna, pasta verde,
polenta, risotto, and crucants (most of the Italian Americans in my town
were descendants of Lombardy); the occasional white-tailed deer, quail,
wild turkey, Canada goose, bluegill, and catfish; red, black, and purple

raspberries, strawberries, apples, peaches, pears, blackberries, blueberries, grapes, and cherries—though not always at one sitting.

The bottom quarter of Illinois, where I'm from, is called Egypt or, sometimes, Little Egypt. One explanation is the bounty of its orchards, fields, lakes, and rivers: one year in the nineteenth century the upper Midwest had a bad winter then lost its crops the following summer, and it was saved by milk and honey from southern Illinois. Others say the name refers to the Promised Land imagined by African Americans fleeing the Reconstruction South. Newcomer Chicago spread the rumor with her wild-onion breath that Little Egypt is a gaunt-cow and locust-plagued wasteland.

The area is a geologic anomaly. Pleistocene glaciers that ground down most of Illinois never arrived. So, while southern Illinois didn't get the utterly flat yet fertile farmland of upstate, it kept its enormous sandstone bluffs and rock formations, such as the odd "streets" between building-shaped rocks at Giant City. Teeming with flora and fauna that in some cases look positively Jurassic, it's part Ozark plateau, part coastal plain of an ancient inland sea. Streambeds and highway cuts are full of fossilized ammonites, corals, sponges, Archimedes' screws, and trilobites as well as the fossil ferns, grasses, and other swampy plants that sprouted and died over the Pennsylvanian Period and became bituminous coal.

The local economy boomed along on that high-sulfur coal for a couple of decades, then went bust and never recovered. It hasn't been easy. The people of southern Illinois are warm and suspicious, often silent but as easily voluble, and natural storytellers. Having been away a while, I'm the least funny one in the bunch.

I wanted Starbuck to know all this, just for context. Then we would drive past all the places of my childhood, and I would say, There, my boy—you see? across that field spotted with lightning bugs?—there I used to make hot-air balloons with my best friend, Eric, out of plastic sheeting and pie plates, and release them after dark. They were mistaken for UFOs, and we listened to a CB radio and giggled as drivers in the vicinity shouted and swore over the airwaves. Eric's dad was an electrician at the mines, a huge man with swollen fists, and he and his tiny wife had four big sons. The family sometimes lived on aid when Eric's dad was laid off again, but because he was a mechanical genius, they owned an airplane, dirt bikes, a dune buggy, a motorboat, and cars too exotic to identify in mid-America back then—Saabs, Peugeots, Jaguars, Porsches, and one of those little cars with its only door in front, between the headlights. It sat in the woods out back, waiting its turn to be restored in the building they all called The Shop. Eric's dad had a heart attack in his Piper on the approach to our local airport, and his quiet tiny wife had to land the plane herself. She clipped a light pole on descent but rolled up safely with her dead husband next to her.

Problem is, I could tell Starbuck whatever I wanted, but he wouldn't retain it. I'm sly enough to show him instead. While we were in southern Illinois, I let him play with friends' kids in the city park where I learned to swim and play tennis. I walked him down several trails through sandstone bluffs at Ferne Clyffe State Park, and we climbed a dry waterfall. College students had stashed empty beer bottles under a boulder at the top of the cliff, and Starbuck wanted to know if they were from, you know, not dinosaur times, maybe, but from ancient times, like back when the cowboys lived, or something . . .

Could be, I said.

He wanted to know why there was a filthy waistband ripped from a pair of underwear up there too, and I said maybe somebody had wanted to go swimming *real bad*. I could see him thinking. We hunted fossils as mosquitoes whined in our ears, and I played music too loud in the car and let him drink all the root beer he wanted on the way home.

This is my pedagogy, which we won't reveal to Mrs. Churm, who sometimes wants to confer on my methods.

Creative Writing
in the Academy

You're right. Writers in the university are often neurotics, and undereducated. They're prima donnas. Their imbalanced juices make them sanguine, choleric, or melancholic, though rarely phlegmatic. I've known a terraphage, a coke hound, and one guy who found his calling after water-skiing into a dock piling. Writers are maladjusted, nearsighted, humpbacked fancy dressers, bare-knuckle fighters and ballroom dancers. Writers are moody and vindictive.

We've got your dog.

Creative writing has always been an awkward fit on campus. Scholars hate writers because writers aren't scholarly; writers resent scholars because scholars impress writers' "texts" as fodder for their campaigns or, worse, ignore them. Also, scholars are seeing writers' ex-wives, and while everybody acts like they're cool with that, they're not.

The act of putting writers in the academy meant, of course, that they needed to be professionalized, the way one professionalizes a cow with an electric prod when it won't get on the cattle car bound for the packing house. Professional demands have escalated, so now it's beginning to take a PhD to get hired, where once it was an MFA, and before that, an MA, and before that, a long cold ride on the rails with the hobos.

Just because you brand an animal as part of the herd doesn't mean it won't gallop off alone for the nearest waterhole at the first opportunity, such as during the first class meeting. College teaching may be the new patronage in the arts, but writers will be writers, not provosts, and god knows what they're telling your kids. They should be teaching in convict settlements or madhouses.

Despite all this, properly run creative-writing classes, sheerly by accident, have become the keepers of the flame of true knowledge in academe. O! you future hog cloners, microchip designers, traders in wheat; players of the football with your husky, brawling big shoulders! Come to Introductory Narrative Writing and sing so proud to be alive under the terrible burden of destiny!

As a younger man I used to ask students, "Why did you come to college?" expecting to hear them quote Hegel, perhaps: "Education is the art of making man ethical." What they told me was, "To learn to do my own laundry." I was deeply hurt. Now I understand they wanted autonomy in whatever form they understood it.

What better place to catch up on your intellectual autonomy than in the creative-writing classroom, where an author always owns her own work? The responsibility to make something unique and good is hers alone, as she writes her way to an understanding of the one thing I cannot understand for her. Half my job is asking questions of those who can't generate questions, in order to model the will to curiosity.

I did this recently for a student in an intermediate creative nonfiction class with two pre-reqs. She couldn't find enough interest in her own topic to be curious about all the paths leading from it to the infinite world, so I did my thing, using my best material. I could play the Copa with this stuff. When I'd generated enough questions and topics to fill a stadium, I stopped, panting, and grinned in triumph. She looked at me for a moment, then said, "So . . . you want me to write about the airport?"

Because I'm ambitious for them, because I had a bad cold, because I was irritated at my life's energy draining from me uselessly, at the next meeting I told them they had to kick it in, this was the real thing, and they must set themselves free. They bent their heads to their doodling in embarrassment for me. They're all rotten to the core, I decided, don't have it, or won't take the one thing that creative writing in the academy has to offer, the chance to see for oneself.

After class, the young woman brought me her revised stuff, which revealed much hard work and a brilliant developing theme of an immigrant family who'd once worked the earth, living now in the only place they could afford in a new city, under the roar and stink of a Jetway.

To celebrate, I stole the chancellor's car.

Letter to a Former Student Now Graduated

There's Rilke and then there's all the horses' asses with their dubious advice. I think you know by now whom I most resemble, so let's begin.

The title of your e-mail to me this week, "Just a Little Nudge," was alarming. What forgotten deadline for a scholarship letter had passed? What law school was impatiently awaiting my reference for you?

I was relieved to read that you thought *you* needed the nudge:

> I've been dancing around the idea of trying to write a book for the last few years; I was noticeably unprepared for the task in your class, but I honed my schedule and workload [and have spent time thinking about] aesthetics, form, etc. I've got (what I consider to be) a great idea, I've built my outline, and I've got a hundred or so pages of notes. . . . But here I am . . . constantly unhappy with what I hear when I read back my work. Am I just not ready yet? Should I look to extend my education and hope that even more coursework will get me there? How is it that you write?

Oh, that. I'm glad you didn't ask about something slightly more difficult, like why the neutral B-meson shows a slight predilection for matter instead of antimatter, forcing our universe's hand to a happy outcome on the matter of being and nothingness.

Writing is easy, actually. Start with the fetishistic:

Never trust your laptop, back up your files often, but if it's served you well through years of constant heavy work, pat its case lightly each time you get up from your labors and say, "Good dog."

Buy several multipacks of that one model of medium-blue ballpoint pen. Best to buy all you can lay hands on, because there's no adequate replacement if the line is discontinued. Leave good spiral notebooks all over the house, one for each project. Be sure the covers are durable, that there are enough sheets, the weight of the paper sufficient, and spacing between lines generous. An astronaut pen in a pocket, always, with refills on hand for when the pressurized cartridges begin to leak, since they always will. A simple small digital recorder in a shirt pocket for car trips or walks. Also a small leather notebook—the kind with the replaceable pads and miniaturized pen that clasps the notebook shut—in a back pocket. Plan for times when you'll have no pockets: swimming, pajama parties, CT scans, lovemaking. What will you do with your writing tools then?

Next, use them to get everything down without regard for quality or usefulness. Sometimes that will mean stepping out of the shower, where so much thinking gets done, and dripping on the cat in order to catch an idea before it runs down the drain. Admire the mythic ruthlessness of Gabriel García Márquez, who it's said turned his family's car around on the way to vacation and drove straight home to write something down. Then he sold the car to pay for time to develop the idea, *One Hundred Years of Solitude*.

Collect all notes from what my wife fondly calls the insanity journals and enter them into a Word document in emotional sequence, which is often not chronological. Begin to build each pointillist jot, in no particular order, and regardless of difficulty, until you see a good reason not to continue with one. Delete the unfit. Sort and rearrange the sequence, listening for connections and the chorale of sense. Have faith. Often it won't be coherent until nearly the end. Cut redundancies. Continue to revise. Again. Again. And again. Yet again. A 500-word blog post, if it hopes to stay news, might need 4,000 words at the start and days of distillation.

There are so many more aspects to the writing that can be seen, one-by-one or together like a nest of pickup sticks, after long practice. But we still have to begin again each time, every visitation bringing new appreciation of the task. Image, for instance, isn't just visual, it's the idea-feeling that short-circuits time and connects self to the world.

The prose informs itself through variety, music, and rhythm. Sensitive performance also suggests the right words, therefore tone and meaning, in the same way that the limerick imposes limits and challenges that lead to it being most itself. Condense to reduce clutter, to elevate intention, and to increase intensity.

When you begin to hear what the piece wants to say, see if you still believe it. If you're working well, you'll be surprised to find you hadn't thought of the thing you most believe. Pause now to read the chapter about disemboweled horses and emotional authenticity in *Death in the Afternoon*.

Listen to the metaphors lying half-hidden in your work. What potential for poetic cohesion do they contain? Those that are seemingly discordant are especially useful. Manipulate them; try minor keys and variations. Build in redundancy and echoes so the reader experiences mild déjà vu, another connection. Endings that emerge from this can be inevitable, surprising, rounded and complete. Remember that Tolstoy says he was stunned when Anna threw herself under the train at the end of his masterwork, even though he'd put her on the train when someone was crushed under its wheels in chapter 1. Mailer calls writing "the spooky art."

Scuff the prose to return a little of its roughness and asymmetry, the way Japanese architects use an awkwardly shaped log somewhere in the design of a milled-timber frame building. This pays a debt to the wildness from which the structure emerges.

Look for chances to simplify without losing anything. "Simplicity is the final achievement," Chopin says. "After one has played a vast quantity of notes and more notes, it is simplicity that emerges as the crowning reward of art."

Leonardo: "Simplicity is the ultimate sophistication."

Longfellow: "In character, in manner, in style, in all things, the supreme excellence is simplicity."

A special note on humor: most writers are not serious enough to be comic. It's often the thing that comes after the final thing, a last reorientation of the crystalline structure, as if a magnet has touched it.

Is there some other craft you could aspire to? Because this one is like stacking marbles.

The good news about writing is that it's the process that makes it. Yes, you should try to become generous, humane, interested, informed, and brave. But in the end you don't have to be the person who writes solid prose. You just have to be the person who chooses to engage fully in the process of writing it. It's like cutting firewood: I don't have to worry about the magic of heat and light that will result. All I have to do is be prepared to swing the maul until the job is done. It's hard, often frustrating work, and it'll wear you out. But there's a satisfaction in finding one's way by process that makes me think of Henry Ford's, "Chop your own wood, and it will warm you twice."

The bad news about writing is also that process makes it. If you're honest with yourself you'll have the humility to defer full credit. Sure, you arrived arm-in-arm with process, and you were there until the end. But process is always the life of the party and has lots of dance partners.

Writing is a need like the body's need to burn energy before it can be at peace. Children kick and flop before sleep; the middle-aged engage in serial affairs and foreclosures; the dying claw their sheets. Are you sure you feel that awful need?

You Shall Know Them
by Their Music

My friend Rory, a university administrator and a poet, is so insistent that writing can't be judged that he uses it as an excuse not to teach: "I wouldn't know what to say to a class," he says, proud of his freedom from the trap of standards. Naturally, he also argues there are neither good nor bad college teachers—only thinking makes it so—and to suggest otherwise is mere advertisement for self.

"Maybe it's my PhD training," he says, "but I see everything as relative."

Privately, of course, he condemns a book as mere "magazine writing," revises his own writing, and, yes, teaches occasionally.

It's nice to be seen as nice, and Chekhov, that saintliest of writers, works passivity into his view of polite society: "Cultured people must . . . respect human personality, and for this reason they are always kind, gentle, and ready to give in to others."

One imagines him nodding gently as the other Moscow doctors who all want to be writers talk him into tubercular coughing fits at dinner parties. (Gorky says, "In [Chekhov's] sad and gentle smile one felt the subtle skepticism of the man who knows the value of words and dreams.")

But in a series of letters to his brother Alex, who wasn't writing to his potential, Anton cracks open like a honeydew:

"Not a single sensible word; nothing but sentimentality. . . . Respect yourself, for heaven's sake and don't let your hand grow slack when your brain grows lazy. . . . Another great authority, Souvorin, writes to me, 'When one writes a great deal, not everything comes out equally good.' . . . I write this to you as a reader having a definite taste. . . . Better poor criticism than none at all. Is it not so?" (Garnett translation)

We can't choose to be free of our individual standards; the question is whether or not we'll discuss them. Unfortunately, I can't retire to my white dacha in Yalta, where I might get the distance to develop a sad and gentle smile. Because I teach I must try to explain myself daily. To do otherwise is a con that some use to buy time to write (or not), taking the pay but not teaching because it's a hassle or because they disdain students.

"I wouldn't do it that way, honey, but you go right ahead," Faulkner is said to have told a writing student under his tutelage. But none of that has to do with the ability to judge good or bad writing.

Discussing one's own techniques and tastes is not dictating them. Indeed, the best teachers I've known could do it while explaining other traditions and encouraging students to situate themselves in the history of ideas. They were not among the massive middle class of American letters that is essentially anti-intellectual. (There is confusion over the term "intellectual" in writing, e.g., the critic who says Hemingway is a "closet intellectual." I mean only, "Given to study, reflection, and speculation.")

What's begun to interest me lately is how quickly an experienced reader can often judge writing. Of course the entire piece must be read, as occasionally even tripe can be skillfully woven, and good work bound in sloppy phrases. (Ever read Dreiser's *American Tragedy*?) But when Rory privately admits he can read the first paragraph of an essay that's come in to the lit journal that he reads for, and know if the rest is worth reading, I don't doubt him. Why, though? It's an important question, since its answers might offer hope for improvement for us all.

"Why" wanders off in every possible direction. Writers who can't or don't care to choose among "to/two/too" don't fill me with confidence, for instance. Sometimes worn-out images, language, or devices are tip-offs; other times it's bombastic diction or confused sentences that stagger around leaking meaning. The reasons may be infinite and depend on the sort of writing attempted, but bad writing does have a look, smell, taste, feel, or sound.

Michael Henry Heim, translator of Kundera, Brecht, Grass, et al., says, in the essay "Translating Chekhov's Plays": "Flaubert once said that the rhythm of a sentence often came to him before the words (and conse-quently before meaning itself). When I first read that, I thought Flaubert was proselytizing art for art's sake or merely exaggerating. But the more I translate, the more I see how right he was: I often find myself fitting words to a pre-existing prosodic pattern."

Musicality in prose is a style of competency. It invites confidence but is not the result of confidence alone; any blockhead is confident. It moves through its own landscape irregularly, surprisingly, but inexorably. (This is no plug for belletrism. Sometimes jagged edges and muscularity are the most beautiful.) What Pound said of poetry applies: "I believe in an 'absolute rhythm' . . . which corresponds exactly to the emotion or shade of emotion to be expressed. A man's rhythm must be interpretative, it will be, therefore, in the end, his own, uncounterfeiting, uncounterfeitable."

It's apparent when the music of a piece of writing has gone flat. Think of Bugs Bunny on the xylophone, incorrectly finishing the phrase from "Endearing Young Charms," to Daffy Duck's utter rage. And it's strange how words can so nearly slip across cultural and linguistic borders in pos-session only of their music. I once saw Robert Pinsky and W. S. Merwin reading from the *Divine Comedy*; original Occitan passages were beautiful even without translation.

This musicality, or its lack, is one of the first things I notice in students' work, and it often parallels the maturity and grasp of the prose. When I read stories by one student I remember well—she's the one I saw, out of the corner of my eye, nodding if I mentioned Austen, Conrad, Jeanette Winterson, anybody—the music played. Sure, sometimes her prose was *marcato* when everything around it suggested *morendo*—she was only about nineteen—but often there were passages of such startling rightness that they were clear as trumpets. She aspired to get the words right, and all I needed to do was encourage and help with control. Some of her peers wanted to be granted the style of Hunter S. Thompson or David Foster Wallace without the hassle of having to understand how sound and sense are fused (or of reading more than one of those author's books), and that simplicity echoed hollowly down the intellectual-emotional halls of the writing.

Students who reach me without having read or written are not too late, but they are delayed. They truly have no standards, so I try to get them thinking about writing, including the basics of hearing words. When a student writes the line of dialogue, "You're such a dick man," he needs help hearing the difference in its rhythm from, "You're such a dick, man," which means something entirely different. In an anxious age that encourages students to be technocrats, not humanities majors, for their own good, it's important to acknowledge openly that there are better and worse bits of writing for as many reasons as we have time to explicate. This is how literacy helps us educate ourselves.

Hardheads

"What are you *working* on?" Crazy Larry said, when I told him about the trees. "Aren't you supposed to be writing about . . . whatever it is you do? You must be a great disappointment to your editor."

He'd called as I was humping to campus with thirty pounds of overdue books and composing in my head: maples are soft, sweet trees that take instruction easily—they're the first to drop everything when cool weather comes in. Oaks are hardheads. Even when forced to take autumn's meaning, they clutch their dead leaves like sheets of foolscap and rustle them until winter's end.

"Maybe it's a poem," I said, breathless from the march to class. "About resistance. That's why we choose oak for the hardest jobs: whiskey casks, gallows, ships of conquest."

"What are you—building an armada in your backyard?" he said suspiciously. "You don't know how to tell a story. Most people don't. In Chicago, they have this black-box theory of theater, all that PC hooey about conflicts and relationships and blah blah blah. Listen, I was at a staged reading last night, and two actresses were making out. I was in the second row and could see their jaw muscles working. Now *that's* drama. They ought to build a whole night of theater around *that*."

~~~

At the mailboxes in the English Department, Rory demanded to know if I'd seen some TV show. "I guess I missed it," I said, absentmindedly flipping through junk. I offered my apology: "We only get about eight channels. Sometimes we watch PBS."

"I'm not like you," he snapped. "What's so great about PBS? I'm not judgmental; an episode of *American Idol* is the same to me as Dickens's *Vanity Fair*. Call me the Postmodern Cowboy."

My creative-writing students often said they were postmodern too. One wrote the relativist sentiment that popsicles and crucifixions were equal; I said it depended on which you were offered. They didn't talk about social construction of the self; that wasn't compatible with the teen ego. They did vaguely admire ideas of their own powerlessness and the impossibility of practical ethics, which made for pretty sweet Thursday nights.

My back, relieved of the pack, tightened up in anticipation of Oronte's Traveling Snake Oil and Talking-cure Emporium. It had been a hard sell all semester. I'd asked them a week earlier to consider a Maupassant short story through the lens of an essay on dramaturgy by John Barth. Half didn't bother, and I'd given them another chance.

They were sitting around the square of tables, looking straight ahead, when I came in. I asked if they were ready to discuss the readings now but saw instantly by their faces that they were still unprepared. *Resistance* is what the educational psychologists call it, and it serves a good purpose: it protects the self, like a shell. Their writing so far had been rants, set pieces, dreams, drug trips—anything but short stories, and it wasn't a beginners' class.

"A story is just a bunch of stuff that happens," one said.

They got angry with me because I suggested a bit of drama with the rant, and an ear for prose. I recalled poet Robert Graves's examiner at Oxford: "You seem to be under the impression, Mr. Graves, that one poem is better than another."

"Our teacher last semester was *nice*," somebody said. "He let us have class outside."

We began workshop. The student story was about some kind of monster (I think) with invisible (?) spikes in its head, who (somewhere) tortures and murders (various unseen) people because he sucks minds (or something). It was written to titillate—the crushing of windpipes the only clear image—a kind of pornography of violence favored by young male students who (I would guess) have never encountered real violence but *love* the idea of it.

"I just wanted to be weird," the author said.

"You succeeded," a young woman said quietly.

I'm paid to make suggestions, so I said: "There's a sister mentioned on page two. Why not use that relationship?"

"You just hate science fiction," another male student said.

My syllabus did say we wouldn't be discussing straight-up genre fiction that brought nothing new to the party, in part to prevent this kind of male fantasy, or its female equivalent, the Bad-boyfriend Romance. I could have rejected it on the basis of not meeting course requirements, but good literature, such as Cormac McCarthy's *The Road*, is often inflected with genre, and I wanted their work to become what it most wanted to be.

"If you want to be weird," I said, "then don't be banal; get *weird*, and make it integral to your story. Make it significant."

I recalled the chapter in *Moby-Dick* where the crew is suddenly surrounded by concentric circles of whales—pods and pods of them—creating a still lake in the middle of the sea, and the men in these little open boats can't harpoon them because they'd be killed themselves in the frenzied panic that would result. In this calm, whales are giving birth and suckling newborn calves. Looking into the depths, the men, in a trance, see uterine blood and whale milk and long loops of umbilical cords like coils of harpoon lines, some with baby whales still attached.

"Like household dogs they came snuffling round us, right up to our gunwales," Ishmael says. "Queequeg patted their foreheads; Starbuck scratched their backs with his lance. . . . Yes, we were now in that enchanted calm which they say lurks at the heart of every commotion."

In a novel about guys out to kill stuff, those life-giving, maternal circles are *significant*.

Who's to say what's significant? the students demanded.

I told them I'd recently driven to Springfield, Illinois, to visit the new Abraham Lincoln Presidential Library and Museum. It's got great exhibits: one long hallway is lined on both sides with dozens of hologram faces, all talking at once about slavery and war and the Union and secession; a waxwork Lincoln, standing dead ahead, looks down at his desk as if he's trying to think in this cacophony. It's effective.

But there are usual, easy stories too: ten-year-old Abe was kicked in the head by a mill horse and lay unconscious all night, and some historians have seized on this event to explain his lifelong "melancholy." Writers in the romance, children's, and sci-fi genres have used it for their purposes, too:

> Abe's long rail-splitting muscles gleamed with sweat as he whipped the mare, the one who'd hurt him, into a froth and imagined a doomed love yet to be. Like maybe Ann Rutledge, who'd promised herself to another man, he thought. That would be *hot*. (*Prairie Fires Burn*, 1982)

> And that kid who ciphered by firelight? That kid kicked in the noggin by a common barnyard animal? It was that kid who went on to be ... President of the United States! And you can too! (*Little Book of Big Presidents*, 1996)

> The horse, an evil robot from space, was sent to doom the puny humans by killing off their great emancipator. But unbeknownst to the Zarkellian programmers, young Lincoln was a robot too, invented by the real Abraham Lincoln, boy scientific genius teleported at birth from nearby Quisp 2, who went on to invent ... an inflatable bladder for refloating grounded keelboats! Manned by *robots*! (*Zarkel's Revenge*, 2002)

Damn lucky robots. If the bad writer could be a robot, too, he would. Machines don't have to feel anything.

Compare those simplistic Lincolns with the deeply moral being that emerges from Carl Sandburg's *Abraham Lincoln*, a weird book that tells how a lawyer saved the world. (I know.) One scene won't leave me, and Sandburg devotes more space to it than to the kick in the head:

When Lincoln was elected, citizens could walk in to the White House to ask the president directly for employment, favors, pardons, and business contracts. They came by the hundreds, adding to his burden. One of them was a woman whose husband and three sons were in the Federal army. With no resources of her own, she'd lived for a while on part of her husband's pay, but that stopped coming, and she needed one of her boys at home.

Sandburg writes, "The President listened to her, standing at a fireplace, hands behind him, head bowed, motionless. The woman finished her plea.

Slowly and almost as if talking to himself alone the words came . . . 'I have two [sons], and you have none.'" He sat and wrote the discharge paper.

But in a few days she was back. She'd found her son dying in a hospital after Gettysburg and had comforted and then buried him. She begged Lincoln for "the next one of her boys." Again, he went to his desk. As if it were all she could do, she followed him across the room, "stood by his chair as he wrote, put her hand on the President's head, [and] smoothed his thick and disorderly hair with motherly fingers."

Can you even imagine such a scene of humanity and humility at another moment in American political life? Lincoln, with that big bony head and awkward body ("Abe-Lincoln ugly" means "strangely beautiful"), so nearly alone, so reviled, denounced as an ignorant rube, in a difficult marriage, a father who'd lost two children to sickness (one in the White House), soon to be shot in the head (as symbolic an act as it was expedient), who faced what no other president has had to, yet retained his compassion.

And that mother: her son and maybe her husband dead; destitute, nearly without hope, standing in the White House, begging for and receiving mercy . . . . She maternally pets the president's dark, unkempt hair, comforting him as if he were her small boy, and she one of the two mothers he lost so early.

Lincoln finished writing, jumped up, thrust the paper at her—"There!" he choked—and strode from the room as she sobbed. I had to be careful with my own emotion as I told it. I get invested in stories, and what would happen if students suspected we weren't instructional machines? There was a long pause.

"I like the robot story better," one of the young guys said. Everyone laughed, and the danger passed.

Matching wits is fun but tiring, and I headed home, tiptoeing through fallen acorns that lay like ball bearings on the pavement. Students are a lot like trees, I thought, of various girths and foliage and densities, and sometimes the ones most resistant to being worked were the best.

I told Frenchy some of this on the phone while I walked, and he considered gravely.

"I got a story," he said. "I knew this navy petty officer, an instructor at the dive school. Every day after work he'd cross the street to the Ten Foot Stop, take a seat on his usual stool, and zip open his fly. He'd pull out a little gold anchor on a chain and throw it on the bar. The other end of the chain was attached to a ring through the head of his dick. 'Keep 'em coming, Jimmy,' he'd tell the bartender. 'I'm moored for the night.'"

⌇⌇

After dinner, Starbuck and I worked on the book he was writing, called *Super Heroes Save the Day Every Day*. I had transcribed the story as he told it, and we broke it down into pages he could illustrate. Chapter 1: "There I was, sitting in my chair in my super room." He drew a stylized asparagus spear. Chapter 2: "Suddenly, a big ghost ship arrived out of the fog to steal my super glasses and laser-finding glasses."

"Should we put a pirate flag on the mast?" I asked, reaching for a black crayon.

"No! No! You're doing it wrong! Dad*DY!*" Starbuck shouted. He stomped to the couch and hid under a blanket printed with a life-size Batman.

"Are we done for now?" I asked him.

"Hmph!" said Batman.

After the kids were in bed, Mrs. Churm and I sat together, reading. She favored a series of novels, each a thousand pages, and was using both hands to hold one to her face. The back cover read: "Their passionate encounter happened long ago. She had traveled back in time and into the arms of a gallant eighteenth-century Scot . . . then returned to her own century to bear his child, believing him dead in the tragic battle of Culloden. Yet . . . her body still cries out for him in her dreams."

Luckily, the rascal's alive after all, so prose like this can exist: "'I said I didna bed with the lasses. . . . I never said I didna look at them. That gown becomes ye. . . .' He cast a glance of general approval at my bosom and waved at a serving maid carrying a platter of fresh bannocks."

The stories were as comforting to her as meat pies with Branston Pickle, and every six months or so, she began again.

"I should put the garbage out tonight," I said.

"Garbage," she said.

As I left the room, I distinctly heard a bodice ripping.

I was thinking hard about the difficulties of story-shaping as I wheeled the bin down the driveway, so I didn't notice the wind gusting and acorns cracking on limbs as they fell. One exploded on the top of my bare head, like a shaped charge.

"Eureka!" I yelled, or something else classical, but no insight came of it. A foreign grad student, getting out of his car at the curb, smiled sweetly at my epithet. I went in the house, nursing my hard head, more determined than ever to tell a story about writing, if only I could find one.

Seeing

One morning back when I was an army deep-sea diver, we were sent down to the port to replace a ship's screws bent by flotsam in the Chesapeake. It was snowing, and we had to drop a fifty-pound weight off the pier to punch a hole in the ice before I could slide into the brown water. When I got under the ship, the big nut on the end of one drive shaft wouldn't come loose, so with a Broco rod hot enough to melt granite and the optimism that her captain would remember not to start the engines and make me his chum, I set to work.

Sergeant Courtly, another diver in the detachment who was the son of a Belizean government minister, sat wrapped in a sleeping bag in our step van back on the pier. He sipped hot cocoa from a Thermos cup, dreamed of his barrier reef, and as if just figuring it all out, pushed the lever on the comms box and said to me down my umbilical: "Jacques Cousteau fucked me up." Then as a joke he turned off my air.

Who wasn't seduced by Cousteau's TV specials? The gleaming *Calypso* is filmed from above by her own dragonfly helicopter, the ship's wake like a comma in the blue water. An underwater shot looks up waveringly at the white hull, and on deck, somewhere near the sun, real men do the things that men do with other real men, while dressed in rubber. Soothing words from the captain in voiceover, then frogmen splay their fins and fall into the sea on clouds of silver bubbles.

What I had seen in all that as a child—and still saw at the age of twenty-two—was a chance to test and prove myself, so now I was under some rusty tub in the James River, working on a case of hypothermia and overbreathing the rig's capacity to deliver air. Sergeant Courtly, who had shed his illusions, sat plotting how to bypass a clerkship in the Ministry of Works and go straight to the Belizean House of Representatives. Who was the fool?

I was thinking about this in my office at Hinterland, a big room with exposed pipes, like the hold of a ship, in which there was the occasional electrical fire. Adjuncts and graduate teaching assistants shared the space, and the gray walls and ancient furniture reinforced the feeling that we were all a utilitarian afterthought. Happily, it did not dampen spirits. Two grad students near the door gossiped about peers who had praised the wrong critic in a seminar; two adjuncts on the couch argued whether the director of rhetoric or the director of graduate studies should be on a calendar they were imagining, to be called the Studs of English. A parliament in the back hooted over a faculty member who got his mistress hired in another department.

Call it proto-scheming: learning social behaviors that will aid them at other highly competitive research universities. I began to feel, like Sergeant Courtly, that I was not in my element. After all, as an adjunct, I was not in any graduate-student cliques, and I wasn't even permitted to *imagine* the secret lives of tenured faculty. Adjuncts may be the lumpen proletariat of the university, but there's a horrible freedom there. Clearly, that attitude wouldn't take me far. By failing to see the need to be engagé, I placed myself at risk of being perceived as a loner, a nonentity, or, in the lingo of hardhat diving, a "waste of O2 [pronounced 'oh-two']," as men once said of Sergeant Courtly.

All of us see wrongly, much of the time, for many reasons: ignorance, animosity, sentimentality, piety, the poisonous effects of that syndicated sitcom where Ted Danson does spit-takes at the counter of some diner, wearing a stethoscope. True seeing requires context, maturity, humor, and a sense of measure.

Take my relationship with the Countess Tolstoy. We raced across the state to rescue her when her time had run out at a shelter, since she was obviously a sweet dog and it wasn't her fault she looked like a beer keg in a yak coat. But at home she sat in the nighttime shadows in our backyard, radiating some creepy vibe that evidently said, "Suffer the little animals to come unto me." And when the possums came grinning to her, crawling under the fence from the dumpster where they ate their last suppers, she clamped her fangs on their spines and shook until their brains came loose. I went through a lot of Ziplocs, turned inside out on my hand, picking up corpses. When I finally got to one I'd missed for a couple of days, its tail came off in my hand. I tried to pick up the rest of it, but the body felt like a wet paper sack filled with rice pudding.

I called Frenchy and began to extol the Countess, what a great watchdog she was, how great she . . .

"She sounds like a fine dog," he said. "I don't want her."

But my squeamishness had blinded me. Our vet said the dog got fresh air, exercise, and a lot of joy from her slaughters, so then I was happy. We all need help seeing properly.

Cézanne sometimes painted in Pissarro's studio, which he described as a place to learn to see. I try to help my students see the possibilities, good and bad, in their words, and I try to bring my own experiences as teacher, reader, writer, deep-sea diver, bus driver, cook, snake handler, father, husband, son, brother, and human being to bear.

One student in my undergrad workshop wrote a short story about a young woman at her first Phish concert. The protagonist saw the best minds of her generation pee in a field, and when she was riding back to Inner Station with her friend, wind tousled her honeyed hair. Suddenly, she felt so wild and crazy and free that she drained the last mouthful of her warm strawberry wine cooler, tossed the bottle out the car window, and it *shattered*. On a *tree stump*. The end.

It's touching—even lovely—that the character, like the author, is sure that no one ever raised hell before that moment. But the story contains no hint that the narrative voice itself knows any better. Its fault is what Emerson criticizes in those who have "no range in their scale": "What is not good they call the worst, and what is not hateful they call the best."

I can help with scale: I knew a guy in a combat engineer battalion who was looking for trouble one night for no other reason than he was an alcoholic and people called him a half-breed, and he tried to get me to fight but I laughed it off, so he went and got the blanket off his bed, soaked it in gasoline, shoved it under the door of a guy down the hall, and lit it on fire so he could burn through the door and get his stereo back.

Now *that* guy knows how to party.

In my literature and rhetoric classes, too, I ask about ways of seeing. What are the limitations, for instance, of the ecstatic worldview of Thoreau? (Frenchy: "That guy went to the woods because he wished to live deliberately, and to pull his pud.") When the burly kid in the John Deere cap insists the black helicopters are on the way (prompted by rhetorical analysis of a speech by Bill Clinton, who may be riding shotgun in the lead chopper), how might our discourse community help him be less afraid?

Facilitating seeing is no small matter. Gertrude Stein wrote, "Gertrude Stein never corrects any detail of anybody's writing, she sticks to general principles, the way of seeing what a writer chooses to see, and the relation between that vision and the way it gets down."

When we write, we unconsciously build ego walls that keep us from seeing "that vision and the way it gets down." There are very few writers, apprentice or professional, who believe they suck. Compare two brief memoirs from *True World War I Stories*, from Lyons Press. Both men no doubt thought they were telling stories well. The first is calm and clear-sighted:

> I landed in France with a medical unit attached to the 7th Division in November 1914. I was a boy just turned seventeen, straight from school, and all the thrill of romance and adventure was on me. . . . There was a wonderful march through the streets of Southampton at midnight, amid crowds of cheering and delirious people. A woman had thrown her arms round me and kissed me, thrusting cigarettes into my pocket. . . . At Poperinghe . . . the casualties poured into the clearing hospital day and night; there was no rest; the smell of blood, gangrened wounds, iodine, and chloroform filled the twenty-four hours. . . . Though often terrified and worn out by the unaccustomed heavy labour, I grew more and more anxious to play my part.

Now listen to the hysterical tone of the second:

> Lark, a weazened, foul-mouthed, little lump of unconscious Cockney heroism, nicknamed under the usual order of such things "Sparrer," lies o' nights

untroubled, I suspect, by any nightmares occasioned by his part in the blood-spewing earthquake of eleven years ago that made his Whitechapel of today fit for heroes to live in. His job done, it is forgotten, except perhaps for periodical arguments in the public bar of his "Local" as to the exact position in Etaples of a certain Red Lamp. Lucky man, may his shadow, always attenuated, never grow less.

I read this to Frenchy, who said, "Hey, I'm no writer, and that wasn't my war. But I've got one word for this guy: Dick. Head."

When it comes to being an effective teacher, the ability to facilitate seeing trumps other matters such as teaching persona, entertainment value, or maybe even interest in students' immediate needs. As an undergrad, I had an English professor who spent two class periods talking about his neighbor's new red car. He tried to quell the inevitable student mutiny—an ugly scene, in which my classmates raged that he wasn't teaching us anything—by declaiming, "Teachers teach. I'm a professor. I profess." (I hope to say that one day at some cocktail party.) But in some fashion I can't explain or defend, he helped me see T. S. Eliot's "Love Song of J. Alfred Prufrock" by topping his car-envy soliloquy with a denunciation of neurotic middle age and a dramatic reading of the poem that included eating a fuzzed peach ("like a young girl," he said), juice dripping off his goatish beard.

Look, it's worrisome that young readers write to me, "I'm thinking of taking the money my parents gave me for tuition and investing it in a Sex Wax concession on the North Shore of Oahu. Oronte, you're an Internet humorist. Do you think I should drop out of college?"

So let me be clear: college forces you (probably) to read, listen to, and consider things you might not have found on your own. That's good. Autodidacts are often eccentrics. And there's a real chance that someone, somewhere, will help you to see. That's as reassuring as the sound of air coming down an umbilical.

Microgeographies

We know most places as we do most people, by mere hints. Accordingly, many believe the state of Illinois is all the same, top to bottom. But if you pulled north-to-south Interstate 57 out of the state like a core sample, you'd see the strata of difference—in geology, topography, biology, culture—between Cairo and Chicago. I've lived in both ends of the state, and I can tell you that the post-industrial city of Chicago peers south past Joliet and sees The Sticks. Down in heavily forested southern Illinois they look north and see only clods.

Central Illinois, stuck between that megalopolis and those Carboniferous uplands, is disdained by both. Yet its open flatness—and the dull uniformity it represents, as if it's a geography of mind—is what most think of when they think of Illinois.

Eighty percent of the state—28 million acres—is agricultural fields. It's not the most hospitable place unless you're a soybean or an ear of corn. Under the depth of the sky, the wind is like a strong underwater current, and ceaseless. In winter the raw damp and frequent ice storms make it seem that the glaciers that ground everything into rock flour have only just receded. Summer heat indices can reach 125 degrees, due in part to the humid breath of crops to the horizon. ("An acre of corn gives off about 3,000–4,000 gallons . . . of water each day," says the USGS.) Dust plumes rise behind the big tractors, and Champaign County is in the nation's worst 10–20 percent added risk of cancer for air pollutants.

But it isn't personal dislike of topography, weather, or flora that hinders understanding. It's that there's hardly an inch that's been *left alone*. What isn't plowed is mowed, and what isn't mowed is ditched, bordered, mulched, or paved. In any case, it's all *owned*, foursquare and police-patrolled, just as it should be. Visitors especially call it rural countryside, but it's more over-determined than any inner city, and a whole lot less anarchic.

The result is that there's almost nowhere to take your ease, to rest, loaf, daydream, dawdle, flop, climb, hide, observe, or even piss in peace. Chicago, now supposedly the "greenest city on the planet," has its public lakefront and parks, its architecture and public art to make life richer. Southern Illinois has many places for contemplation, such as Crab Orchard Wildlife Refuge, Shawnee National Forest, or the banks of two enormous rivers. Central Illinois, midway between forest and city in more ways than one, represents the Industrial Age as applied to agriculture and is both anti-human and antinature. It doesn't even benefit directly from agribusiness cultivation: 75 percent of what's grown goes to cows, cars, and (more) corn, and Illinois must import 90 percent of its food.

Illinois is ranked dead last among Midwestern states for acres protected per capita for conservation and recreation—only 1 percent is owned by the state—and only about two thousand acres of high-quality, relatively undis-turbed prairie, about .01 percent of the original, remain. But as Thoreau famously implied, it's not wilderness so much as wildness that's necessary to our lives, and I'm always looking for small details, burgeoning and fading to their own plan, that will allow me some elemental understanding of a place.

It's as hard to find the salvation of intimacy in shorn fields as it is on the blank face of the sea, but on the edge of that town there's a 130-acre prairie park called Meadowbrook that we used to use for quiet adventures. Two summers I double-dug and tended an organic garden plot there, which taught me many things. Our black Lab, straining on his leash, once flushed nine pheasants from a patch of switchgrass and wild carrot and later that day gobbled a pile of underfur where a rabbit warren had been; he learned of heaven. My wife and I strode along Meadowbrook's concrete paths to induce her labor, keeping eyes open for mole salamanders, wood frogs, trout lilies, snow trillium, and other signs of new life.

That slow taking-in of the natural world, its rhythms, processes, is what I want my sons to discover for themselves. Starbuck was five and interested in science and the natural world, and when I took him to Meadowbrook that spring we followed a swollen stream so he could imagine a beaver's dam at every jumble of flood wrack. We sat in a copse, ate a snack, and pretended to be deer hiding from joggers. A wild turkey called; another responded at great distance. Mourning doves hooted.

At first I took the jumble of bones for a big dog's, but the spine was longer than a man's, the ribs bigger, and the skull had no canines—a real deer then. My son stood somberly a few feet away, despite his great love of dinosaur and other bookish bones, while I snapped a couple of pictures. The skeleton was largely intact, but as we walked on I saw vertebrae and other small bones deposited two hundred yards away by something hungry. I didn't mention them.

Starbuck suddenly wanted every odd noise—rattle of seedpods, screech of bird of prey—explained to his satisfaction. Half a mile away at the edge of the park's big playground, a clumsily laminated sign that had fallen from a post said, "Sorry about the smell." It explained that dead animals were left to rot, unless they posed a danger to public safety, to complete life's cycle for both prairie and people. The sweet stink of education.

By bedtime, my son had tamed the bones and seedpods and raw Illinois wind by putting them into stories of our adventures for his mother and little brother. As I turned out the light, he stretched luxuriously between flannel sheets and heaved a great sigh of satisfaction at his new and valuable knowledge, having seen for himself how lightly uncultivated death sits on our little landscape.

Geedunk and Geegaws

Geedunk (gee'·dunk): 1. Navy word for junk food: candy, ice cream, potato chips. 2. Food or drink as souvenir: two liters of mediocre table red bought in a Monoprix in Paris, carried across two continents in a cardboard wine box with "bon vivant" on the sides, then found cheaper at the Piggly Wiggly in Tulsa.

Geegaws (jee'·jaws): 1. Trinkets and baubles. 2. Useless souvenirs, often fragile or unwieldy, though not necessarily cheap: a porcelain figurine with tiny arms and hands, waving a feathered cavalier hat; a book in the size known as "double elephant folio"—50 inches high and heavier than a baby stroller—containing color plates of Monrovia.

Mrs. Churm caught me gazing at old photos of bachelor adventures and sniffing the suntan lotion. Ignoring my hints that I use our air miles to fly to Nepal, she asked if I wanted to visit Frenchy, who was renting a condo on Snowshoe Mountain and building his log house a couple thousand feet below the lodge.

"That would be *great!*" I said, then saw the look on her face and added, "I *am* on deadline for that magazine piece; this would give me time to finish. And I'll bring you and the boys something nice."

"You don't need to get me anything," Mrs. Churm said, and I knew I'd better bring her something extraordinary.

~~~

A tale about geegaws: A friend wanted to see the Three Gorges before the deluge. Somewhere up the Yangtze, he, his wife, and fellow passengers debarked at a village market selling the usual teapots and brass bells and cans of Chinese soda. My friend spotted something unusual in the back of a stall; a girl said it was a poncho, used when her grandfather worked the fields. My friend looked at the ratty, rotting thing—apparently made of bark—and asked if it was for sale. The girl wanted a few bucks for it.

"You are *not* buying that," his wife said.

Now it meant something, you see.

"I think I *will* buy it," he said.

"If you try to buy that hideous thing I'll go back to the boat alone," she said.

"See you back at the boat," he said cheerfully.

Before the transaction was finished the boat's whistle blew, and a state senator from Minnesota, traveling free because his wife was the tour agent, bellowed that my friend should be left behind. But he got his poncho.

His wife refused to sleep with it in their cabin, so he wrapped it lovingly in a garbage bag, stowed it in a locker in the steward's galley, and checked on it in the night. He got trench foot on his hands from carrying the sweaty plastic through airports and endured vigorous probings by security agents because he couldn't explain what he was clutching. On the airplane he put it in the overhead; his wife moaned that its proximity was going to make her vomit, until he began to feel queasy, too. Finally, he took it to their Chinese hotel's business center, handed them his credit card, and said, "Ship it. I don't care what it costs."

Two months later, when it got to their house, he figured out that, with exchange rates for its purchase, and special packaging and shipping fees, and the insurance he didn't ask for, he'd paid, oh, *a million dollars* for it. His wife demanded to spend the same on herself as recompense for all she'd suffered, and he agreed, to make peace.

The best part: Go visit them sometime. She'll answer the door in a Mandarin dress, her hair pinned up with chopsticks, and ask if you'd like to see the really cool bark poncho they bought in China, which she hopes to have someone from the Art Institute appraise. He'll pretend to be finding pictures from their trip and won't say a word. Who says geegaws aren't important?

~~~

With the semester over, I drove into a June sunrise, the trunk filled with books, rooster sauce, fish sauce, good wine, and better bourbon. Ohio was under construction, but West Virginia rewarded me with black cows grazing in lush grass up to their hocks on a hillside; the forested ridge behind them glowed with sun. A bit further into the mountains, near Nutter's Road, I lost my cell signal for good. Here, I thought, is where I'll go all Kurtz, train battalions to explicate and parse as we sip sumac tea and gobble tiger-lily blooms. I'll compose essays in nut shells and tail feathers, and Dennis Hopper will deliver them to my editors, on an ass.

I stopped daydreaming at Flinderation Road, the start of the Land of Roadside Crosses. The sunset in my mirror turned the color of the apocalypse, then it started raining. A sign offered "Deer Cutting." Fog rolled down the mountains onto the road. Night fell, and it rained harder.

In a dark hamlet I stopped at the last Hardee's on earth and dashed inside to ask directions. I was still wearing the clothes I'd left in: white shorts, the yellow polo shirt Mrs. Churm bought me for my birthday, and running shoes over Nautica anklets (desperation socks; my others were packed). Cowboys waiting for their Angus burgers stared, puzzled how I'd gotten there from Pluto.

It only took five hours more to climb Frenchy's driveway. I'd been saving my liver for old age, but he built up the fire and we talked a long time. Then I slept without stirring in the cold air from the open window. I woke after dawn to omelets cooked in bacon drippings, biscuits with butter and elderberry jelly, and black coffee.

~~~

What the semioticians call signs—cultural artifacts invested with meaning—can be seen everywhere, from the socks we choose to the "Monster Thickburgers" (1,420 calories) we eat. A ski resort is a sign, too. Life on a mountaintop requires such tremendous resources—to fight exposure, maintain infrastructure, and haul flavored syrups up to the Starbucks—that for much of history it's been shepherds, ascetics, and the foolhardy who chose it. It still connotes separation, now more likely to be between rich and poor.

Snowshoe is such a commanding presence—economically, physically, politically—that it does as it likes. What it likes to do occasionally is flush overflow sewage into waterways that run to the towns, where the resort's own minimum-wage service-industry workers live. Frenchy probably wouldn't like the place at all if it weren't for its skiing, restaurants, shops, views over the Alleghenies, barbecue and jazz festivals in the summer, and the conversation of the bartender in the boathouse at the bottom of the lift. ("You know how it is: you meet a guy, and you got to go with him," she explained to us.)

Each morning, I worked in the condo while he hung doors and cut molding in his house down on a tributary of the Elk River. He was planning a bigger house for the upper slope of his meadow, which was covered with foxtail, teasel, and Montrose rose. Indigo buntings looked in his windows, and the hawthorns were in bloom. Afternoons we sanded and stained, inspected other people's land, or went caving. Every night we drove back up to the condo and feasted without end.

One night, after a run to town for groceries and a copy of the *Pocahontas Times*, I read an article on eighty-one-year-old Jake Hilleary, who used to trap bears for the state. Once, he brought some clay to get a bear's paw print.

"I wanted to make me an ashtray," he said.

He was "straddling the [sedated] bear and pushing its front paw into the clay that [he] was going to get baked in Johnnie Hill's kiln," when his coworker gave the bear the antidote for the tranquilizer.

"He just got up and took off with me on top," Jake said. "He took me right to the woods. . . . I guess I'm the only one in the state that ever rode a wild bear."

Well, sure. In the *state*.

Geedunk and geegaws are signs at the intersection of two worlds. A plastic mug bought at the city zoo, injection-molded to look like a panda, brings together the cloud forest and the concrete jungle. To the buyer it says, "I appreciate the wondrous diversity of species on this small blue planet, and bubble-gum-flavored snow cones."

Souvenirs commemorate difference in forms entirely safe (if they don't carry you to the woods) and freed from context. That's why they're so often grotesque (alligator-head key chains in Florida) or tacky (candy cigarettes in the Stuckey's of my youth). A bark poncho in a museum-quality frame, hung on the wall with a couple's wedding photos, means something to (and about) its owners, even if it's as cryptic as a word carved in a tree in Roanoke.

<hr />

On my last day in West Virginia, Frenchy and I cooled beer in the river and tossed canned corn to the trout. He told me about his neighbors. One old man had told the county he'd be on his porch with his shotgun if they wanted to come by to hook him up to the sewer system that Snowshoe was forcing through.

"You'll fit right in here," I said.

"I come from a long line of hard bastards," he agreed. "My great-grandmother Molly's first husband went to Florida to drain swamps. He died working, and the crew left him on the side of the road. Molly went for his body her*self* and took it home to Alabama. Later she married a man named Finnegan, my great-grandfather. Now he was Irish, so he liked to *drink*. But Molly towered over his *ass*, and she'd go *after* him. He'd run to their bed and pull the sheet over himself, quaking, and yell, 'Molly! *In your wrath, remember mercy!*'"

The next morning I packed to go home. The sun warmed clouds lying in the hollows, and they rose like wraiths and were shredded by the breeze. We shook hands and I flew down the mountain. Robins bathed in frigid water in the ditches along the falling road between the trees. Ahead were more mountains, and I drove down and up for hours before rolling out on the plains.

I knew I was back in my usual world when Crazy Larry called. He was in his car too and shouted that while I was away he'd been denied rush-hour entertainment. I told him I had bigger problems: in every store in West Virginia the black-bear knickknacks had been molded in Colorado, the apple butter processed in New York, and the toys manufactured in Taiwan. Where were the locals' wood carvings, the irregular thrown pots and amateur landscapes, the slippery-willow flutes? Soon, I said, the only geegaws in America with discernible differences would be mass-produced T-shirts bearing logos of various corporate resorts.

"Why do people want to save old ways of life?" Larry interrupted. "Certain things are meant to disappear, like all that stuff you said. Or telephone operators. People are dumb enough to wish we had *them* back. Same with family ranchers and farmers. I saw some of them on TV, the big babies. Listen, I *want* Walmart and Best Buy and Chili's to run everything for me. I *want* everything to be the same. I want to be sealed in a Twinkie the size of a living room and live there for*ever*."

I said we needed to know about different things such as finishing houses and making Vietnamese noodle soup in order to have metaphors with which to think comparatively, maybe even empathetically.

Larry said, "You're gonna have to explain this empathy thing to me someday."

I told him my theory about souvenirs as little talismans that we buy because they reassure us we can survive difference. I told him about the cowboys in Elkins stunned by my clothes, which were signs of foolish disregard for weather and landscape.

Larry said, "Maybe they were just wondering why a guy was wearing Nautica anklets ten years out of fashion."

I paused long enough that he thought we had lost the cell signal.

"Hello?" he said.

"How's your bark poncho?" I asked.

~~~

Halloo, the house! I'm back, Mrs. Churm! Bring in the boys—hello, boys! Come see the marvels I brought you: a fossil calamite in limestone, coal from the tender of a logging train, a rusty spike that once held its rail to the earth. I see you eyeballing all the regulation geedunk and geegaws, Mrs. Churm, and, yes, here's a jug of West Virginia maple syrup, three T-shirts, two toy animals, and a comically large lollipop. But I also brought home my gratitude and desire, and more stories than I can tell my love, you.

Move-In Blues

Astrophysicists must have a term for the chaos that exists when individual bodies in mutually influential orbits haven't settled into equilibrium. I call it move-in week.

It's not a problem everywhere. In Miami, where the city is a giant gateway for transience anyway and the university relatively small, the arrival of students in the fall is unnoticeable. But in Inner Station we lost about a fifth of the town's population each May 15, got used to having those thousands gone, then saw them wash back up at the end of August.

On Freshman Move-in Day you could hear them coming, before they ever left Chicagoland, like barbarian hordes from the North. Dads everywhere were seething with rage that despite all good intentions the tribe was starting later than planned. Moms were still vacuum-bagging comforters at midmorning, all the kids had gone to Target for last-minute earbuds, and all those dads sat in their SUVs in their driveways, racing their engines to red line to make their point.

I walked over to campus to take a look. Signs stuck in the ground outside the nearest dorm read, "20 Minutes to Unload and Go" and "Unattended Cars May Be Relocated." A young woman named Karen in a shirt that read "Hall Chair" had command of an army of orange-shirted I-Guides, whose task it was to drag in arrivals' belongings on flat dollies. She gave one of them a thumbs-up, then spoke to someone on her walkie-talkie. I asked her how things were going, and she said there hadn't been much of a rush yet.

"Looks like the rain is letting up now, though," she said cautiously. We'd been a long time without rain; even the hostas around the building were drooping and dusty.

The university had let some students into dorms earlier in the week, but traffic for this dorm was still routed around several city blocks, with monitors, police, and students who would hand out free stuff placed strategically along the route. In the hour I stood watching, none of that was necessary. A dozen minivans, official car of the American middle class, were parked at the curb in front of the main entrance at any given time, but there was no line of traffic waiting, and families got checked in, dropped off, and moved along quickly.

"If you ladies are in group one, you can go on downstairs after this load," Karen told a few of her troops. "Travis, do you need help?"

Families dragged in all the stuff needed to survive a semester at a big state university. It was packed in Sterilite bins, Texaco antifreeze boxes, laundry baskets, laundry bags, garbage bags, Dell computer boxes, plastic filing cabinets, Office Depot sacks, Container Store containers with more containers inside them. A dad ran through the drizzle with a flat-screen TV held protectively in his arms like a baby. Nearby a member of the campus workers' union stood under a large tree, watching, not bothering to hold up his protest sign that read "Justice for All." He looked at his watch and left.

It began to rain again, hard. A mom stood at the back of a minivan, yelling, "La maleta," at her husband's rump as he dug around in the dry interior.

"Eh?" he said.

"La maleta! La maleta!" she cried over the hiss of water. Next to her on the sidewalk was stacked case upon case of bottled water, canned energy drinks, and Shin cup noodles. Karen was instantly on the scene, her hair plastered to her head now.

"How many you expecting today?" I said when they were done and Karen had taken shelter under the overhang at the entrance.

"A hundred and thirty families," she said.

"How many are still left?" one of her soaked orange-shirts asked ruefully.

It rained harder, a real downpour now, and another orange-shirt down the dripping line called loudly and cheerily, "Welcome to the university!"

The thought of those 130 little tribes made me blue, not because they would invade our town but because everything about the university, from its landscaping and architecture to the education it provided, to its organizational efficiency, would have the effect of distancing, for a time if not permanently, the members of those tribes. I was one of those who helped make it happen, and I felt a little sorry for that power.

～～

The start of classes meant even more social confusion. Foot, bike, skateboard, scooter, and car traffic was swarming and disorganized enough to be dangerous. That young driver down from Winnetka had been taught not to let pedestrians bluff her; those students talking excitedly as they sauntered across the street weren't about to be intimidated by dad's matador red, two-ton Lexus SUV. It's the principle of the thing.

The annual infusion of students to any college town provides literal rejuvenation, "renewal of youth," and it's nice to think that university employees—like drill sergeants, McDonald's store managers, and others who work with those eternally eighteen to twenty-two years old—might stay mentally young as a result. The reality is that many who grow physically old serving students also get crotchety at their return.

Crazy Larry, whose day job is at another Big Ten school, was incensed enough by an accumulation of rude student behaviors that he called me to complain. He'd been standing in line at a supermarket near campus, waiting to pay for his Snickers bar, I guess, when an undergrad cut in line and leaned too close to pick up a shopping basket at Larry's feet.

"I said loudly, right in his ear, 'Excuse me!'" Larry told me. "He didn't even acknowledge he heard me, let alone offer an apology. He got his basket and began to walk away, and I saw he had a hint of a grin. So I shouted, 'Well, excuse you!'"

"Good one," I said.

"What?" Larry demanded. "Their parents don't teach them manners, and they're going to need to know how to coexist with others in a civilized society. I was giving him something valuable," he said pedagogically. "It doesn't matter to me, but it's the principle, you know?"

There was a lot of sudden shouting where I was, too, both angry and joyful, that wouldn't occur after everyone settled into routines. I was worried by a girl who sat on the curb, weeping into her cell phone, but apparently she was yelling at her boyfriend, who'd been left behind only twenty-four hours earlier and was already suspicious she'd met someone. College makes a palimpsest of students' former lives, and many will be overwritten entirely.

What always surprised me most during this time was the enormous quantity of junk and trash that emerged, evidence of sudden change on the American landscape. Leases were up, summer tenants had left, and old houses near campus looked as if they'd been turned inside-out. Victorian painted ladies started to look like Baby Jane, their open doors and windows perfuming the town with dankness and rot.

The curbs through those neighborhoods were lined with pee-stained twin mattresses, broken bookshelves, desks, and other particleboard disposable furniture, kitchen chairs, chunks and crumbs of Styrofoam, rusty grills without lids or handles. Broken windowpanes, a half-sheet of drywall with hammer holes punched into it, old shoes singly and in pairs, a toilet dethroned. Junk rolled back from the street in piled-up waves and flattened onto lawns like surf on a beach. Cardboard packing boxes lay at the curb and next to dumpsters, in stacks like decks of cards or toppled over and pushed into the mud, along with takeout boxes from the pizza it took to get them unpacked. New appliance boxes, for a Cuckoo rice cooker, a Target floor lamp, a Pharaoh's bong. Used condoms and crushed beer cans. The unwrapped news of the day. Turkey vultures, new to the area, soared at treetop, riding thermals on six-foot wings and hoping to take a closer look. Squirrels, sated with crusts and rotten fruit, lay flattened on low branches and fences with disturbing come-hither looks.

I stopped by the Foreign Language building to see my friend Mike and was trapped by another tropical downpour. When I was finally able to leave two hours later, water was still pouring through overhead cracks in the long plywood tunnels meant to shield students from renovation debris. Storm drains had been overwhelmed, the streets were flooded, and all the junk and garbage on the curbs was sodden and melting. Added to it now was the jetsam at the high-water mark: broken branches, twigs, walnut shells, clumps of oak leaves that had been flimsy squirrel nests, bottle caps, pieces of roofing shingles, student schedules, campus maps. Nature brought cleansing rain, but it would take man to clean up man's mess.

That weekend was fine and clear, and my family was finally able to go flying with Mike, who owned a historic light plane he kept in a hangar in the next town. We flew over Inner Station and got permission to orbit the quad and then our house, so the kids could tell their friends. Things looked a lot less cluttered and confused from 2,400 feet.

On the return to the country airfield Mike offered me the stick for a moment, my first time at the controls of an airplane. I found it was much like piloting a boat; you have to look off into the distance to gauge your actual course, since the sensations of movement are misleading. I aimed for a water tower on the horizon that stood near the landing strip but kept overcorrecting one way then the other, making the Piper yaw lightly back and forth, and I'd have to learn to maintain altitude another day. As the sun rose, thermals developed over the patchwork quilt of corn and soybeans, and the flight got progressively hotter and bumpier. Wolfie started looking queasy in the backseat, but it was nice to be together for a time and headed in the same direction.

The Recipe in the Writing Class

In the past my creative nonfiction class has focused on times and places important to students' lives—memoir, but with an emphasis on looking outward more than in. Students did excellent work, but I wasn't satisfied with the class, if only because it became the occasion for one young writer to get liquored up and take the train to interview an ex-boyfriend, whom she said she'd hurt badly, to draw fresh blood. I started thinking of changing the focus to food writing instead. I suppose a student might get liquored up and take the train to tell mom her beef stew is greasy, but someone needs to after all.

There are many approaches to writing well about food, from journalism to memoir to political and cultural histories. The best, going back to that of Jean Anthelme Brillat-Savarin, the Montaigne of food, is both thoughtful and evocative. Some writers, such as A. J. Liebling in *Between Meals*, make food a fetish. Others, such as Maupassant in his short story "Boule de Suif," use it as backdrop and motif for drama. The very best, such as Isak Dinesen in "Babette's Feast," treat it as a human need as soulful as love.

The temptations of the form are there in its function: mastication is a private act, even when done in public, and food writing can easily become onanistic. The worst of the memoirish genre is set in the eternally bronze glow of the setting sun of a distant land, the prose purple and flowery, and reading it is like eating gloppy pasta al forno soaked in lavender perfume.

M. F. K. Fisher, born one hundred years ago, is known as a food writer, but she said she wrote of hunger. The *New York Times* wrote, "In a properly run culture, Mary Frances Kennedy Fisher would be recognized as one of the great writers this country has produced in this century." I use her essays even in fiction classes. For Christmas I got the fiftieth-anniversary edition of her *The Art of Eating*, a 740-page collection of several earlier books including *Serve It Forth*, *Consider the Oyster*, and *How to Cook a Wolf*.

It's this last one, written in 1942, that provides an interesting nonfiction form I might call The Recipe, which got me thinking about how to restructure my nonfiction course. The book was written when wartime shortages had compounded the problems of the Depression, and Fisher offers sensible advice in each chapter about how to make do, provide nutrition, and even enjoy oneself at table. Along the way she illuminates her times.

For true emergencies, the essay "How to Stay Alive" ponders what's needed spiritually and nutritionally to survive on what was a few cents a day in her time. It includes a recipe for making a slumgullion of "ground whole-grain cereal," a tiny amount of cheap meat, and loads of vegetables ("wilted and withered things a day old maybe . . . [or] the big coarse ugly ones"), stewed three or more hours:

> I know, from some experience [that it] holds enough vitamins and minerals
> and so on and so forth to keep a professional strong-man or a dancer or even
> a college professor in good health and equable spirits. The main trouble with
> it, as with any enforced and completely simple diet, is its monotony. It must
> be considered, then, as a means to an end, like ethyl gasoline, which can never
> give much esthetic satisfaction to its purchaser or the automobile it is meant
> for but is almost certain to make that automobile run smoothly.

All this sounds more applicable with each morning's news.

Each chapter of *How to Cook a Wolf* contains one or more recipes, a self-imposition on form, like rhyme in poems, that Fisher doesn't usually use in her work. In the introduction to *Serve It Forth* (1937) she says, "Recipes in my book will be there like birds in a tree—if there is a comfortable branch." Even when she stops a story and starts a recipe, she's just continuing in another mode, since her recipes are also full of commentary, explication, and metaphor. On baking bread: "From there on, when you first assemble the ingredients, the dance begins. It is one that should be rehearsed a few times, probably, but I know that it can be done with astonishing if somewhat frenzied smoothness the first time."

To the degree that writing imitates organic forms, an absence of perfectly straight lines can be as desirable as symmetry, balance, and functionality. Fisher's work always has these virtues, its most literary quality apart from her perfect pitch and ability to spot story. Her essays start where she needs them to, end when she's said what she wanted, and are as inevitable as they are unexpected.

If I did have a nonfiction class write about food, I'd go heavy on Fisher in the reading and ask students, at least once, to extend comfortable branches for a few birds to nest in their trees.

～～

Here's my own try:

My brother-in-law's grandfather was kind and had an infectious laugh, but he was also a tough old bird, and to watch him eat was to be shown what he'd endured in his time. As a young man he'd been a machine-gunner in World War I, which he spoke of as a life's adventure, and when he came home he went straight to the mines and then the munitions factory. He was middle-aged in the Depression, in already-depressed southern Illinois.

Most holidays we all sat at his daughter's kitchen table, with him at the head. He'd load up his plate—once—with everything to be had: celery with cream cheese, pickles, olives, baked ham, turkey, mashed potatoes and gravy, baked beans, southern green beans, dumplings, rolls and butter, cranberry salad, baked yams, and more. After grace he dug in. He didn't race through his meal, but he never spoke either and applied himself to the bounty with a will, pausing only to sip iced sweet tea. He ate seriously and pleasurably, looking at the food, and when it was gone—he never took second helpings—he used his last bite of bread to mop up the juices on his plate, and ate that too. Then he was done and seemed to come to, or come back from somewhere else.

The holidays have always reminded me of other generations' attitudes about food. My mother, a child of the Depression, always made sure our Christmas stockings each contained an apple, an orange, and a handful of nuts in shells, along with the more pleasing chocolates, candy canes, toys, and coloring books. I thought of the fruit and nuts as mere filler and knew the fun was over when I got to the heavy lump of the orange in the toe of the sock, but she'd inhale its fragrance deeply and comment on the fruit's perfection, so I came to associate it with the miraculous. Even now I insist that Santa put those items symbolically in our boys' stockings, though we've never faced citrus shortages or prohibitive cost in the supermarket, any time of the year. (Unshelled nuts are still a bit exotic: no one wants to bother.)

New Year's supper is the final and the homeliest of these winter traditions. We'll want great northern beans with ham, best made from scratch, boiled with stock, vegetables, and bay leaves until they thicken themselves, and served with sweet cornbread. My Aunt Margie was the one who made them in our family.

My mom always said that Margie, an artist, started married life around World War II knowing how to cook only two things: fudge and spaghetti. Twenty-five years later Margie had added to her repertoire, mostly sweets that even as a kid I never really liked: strawberries hand-molded from Rice Krispies and chopped dates, rolled in red granulated sugar, and topped with bitter little green frosting stems; crescent cookies with almost no sugar in the dough but a blanket of powdered sugar on top that was easy to breathe in and choke on; and crumbly shortbread balls that were really an apologia for unexcellent butter. Spaghetti remained popular as a main course, as I remember, and the fudge was always tooth-achingly sweet and good, if a little granular. When she grew older and the husband she'd tried to cook for had died, Margie dined like an ascetic, on toast and cups of hot tea, as if acknowledging she'd been a culinary poetaster all along.

Still, some of my fondest food memories are from her kitchen, where there was a large round oak table with a lazy Susan that encouraged family-style meals and long talks, at which even the youngest had an equal role. My grown cousins taught me to play card and board games in that kitchen and let me taste kosher wine. At New Year's, Margie's great northern beans and ham bubbled on the stove until a light crust formed on top and starchy drippings baked hard down the side of the pot. Margie said every bean you ate that day was a dollar you'd earn in the new year, though an exact figure could never be calculated since she'd boil them until their atoms recombined to make a motile sludge that grumbled and steamed like a banker.

Never pin your financial hopes on a legume. Ham and beans is really about making use of what one already has at hand, driving one's own good luck by not wasting opportunities, such as a few handfuls of hard beans and the inedible shank of a pig left over from Christmas dinner. It's food for the poor, who dream of dollars one at a time. If ever there was an adjunct's dish, this is it.

Enjoy a bowl this New Year's. I've updated her recipe so even the tenured will like it.

Recipe for Instant Karma Beans

> 1 lb. bag of dried great northern beans
> Leftover ham bone, with any meat still attached
> 2 or 3 cans low-salt chicken broth
> 1 medium onion, diced
> 1 rib of celery, sliced thin
> 1 large carrot, peeled and chopped
> 1 tbsp. olive oil
> 2 bay leaves
> ½ tsp. baking soda
> Salt and black pepper to taste

Rinse and pick over the beans. Soak overnight in cold water. Drain and rinse.

Make a stock by bringing the ham bone to a hard boil in enough cold water to cover it. Skim foam and impurities during first 10 minutes. Add bay leaves, reduce heat, and simmer 3–4 hours, topping with chicken broth as needed to replenish what boils away. The stock will need to be salty in the end to flavor the bland beans, but if it starts to get overpowering, top up with water instead of chicken broth. Some people like to add a little brown sugar, but there's no need if the ham was glazed. (Glaze will impart cloves and spice too.) Remove the bone and bay leaves when done. Pick the bone for any shreds of meat and return them to the stock. Discard bone and bay leaves.

Sauté the onion, celery, and carrot in the oil until the onions are translucent. Add this mirepoix, the beans, and baking soda to the stock. Add water or broth as you see fit. Bring back to a boil, then simmer for at least an hour or until the beans begin to fall apart and their own starch starts to thicken them slightly. Pepper to taste; start with a lot and go from there. You could also use white pepper if you don't want to sully the beans' color, or cayenne. Or let people add their own hot sauce at table.

The dish should be somewhere between soup and a stew. If the consistency rounds the corner to look like porridge, you might as well stick an immersion blender in it and blend it all smooth. No harm done. Serve with buttered cornbread and a glass of cold milk, and meditate on what just rewards would look like if luck were on your side. . . .

A Remembrance of
Gravies Past

In the same way that our radio and TV broadcasts will apparently bounce around forever in the physical universe, many things that fragment and grow faint in the mind don't disappear entirely. They can be retrieved, if you have the right equipment and can find a quiet place to listen.

At the rehearsal dinner before a recent wedding, I sat next to my cousin Shirl and her husband, Hank, and was overcome with childhood memories long forgotten: attending Shirl's graduation from Southern Illinois University (a master's in piano, so lovely and impractical in such a place) and being allowed to take photos with Hank's professional cameras. Mopping the floors of Hank's photography studio after his partner ran off with their money and he tried to keep the business afloat. Feeling sorrier when Hank burned down part of his mother's house warming frozen pipes with a blowtorch and, later, using my toy metal detector to look for Shirl's wedding ring in the charred wreckage of their own house after Hank had thawed those pipes. They took me to a Buckminster Fuller lecture, tricked me into eating beef tongue, and lived on a fallow farm not far from SIU's Touch of Nature Environmental Center. In complicated ways, they're important to my sense memory of the 1960s.

As we chatted, I remembered one event so clearly it was like having a flashback. My mom and I had gone to an aunt's house—Shirl's mom and mine were sisters—and Shirl and Hank sneaked me a comic book called *Primal Man?* Most of my comic books at home were hand-me-downs from my sister: Richie Rich, Caspar, Little Dot, Little Lotta, and Wendy the Good Little Witch. This was something new.

The front cover said it was "Volume 6" of a series called *The Crusaders*, and it showed an enraged mastodon attacking a caveman, who was about to fall off a cliff into lava. The artwork was grotesque, garish, and violent. The back cover listed profiles of the two main characters: Tim Clark, "Ex-Green Beret, he met someone in the jungles of Viet Nam who changed his life," and James Carter, "Ex-crime boss, he ruled the streets in Chicago, until he met his match." Cool, I thought, and crept behind the couch, out of the gaze of my mother, to learn how a Green Beret would deal with a mastodon. ("Caution: This set of books could change your life," the comic book said.)

Greedily, I began to read. By page eight, the battle between Borg and the mastodon is revealed to be a movie in production. Our two heroes, Clark and Carter, have gone to the set to meet their old chum the lead actor, handsome under his caveman mask. They bring with them "Dr. Lind," who tells the movie's director, producer, and moneymen (from the "International Geographic Commission"), "I believe evolution is one of the cruelest hoaxes ever invented!" Their responses are, variously, "What the?", "Gasp!", and "Hey . . . who is this joker?" When the film's science advisor says, "Dr. Lind . . . you don't believe that God created the universe, do you?", Lind testifies that he does, and someone says, "I bet he even believes in Mickey Mouse . . . and that wierd [*sic*] little old tooth fairy! Haw Haw Haw!"

The grownups in my aunt's living room were droning to each other in the uninteresting way they do, but I heard Shirl ask my mom offhandedly, "You and Oronte want to come to a dinner tonight?"

"To dinner? Or *a* dinner?" my mom asked suspiciously.

"A dinner."

"What kind of a dinner?"

"Oh, it's for our church," Shirl said. "We'll have a speaker, and it'll be fun. It's at the student center at SIU."

In the comic book, the crusaders are working out on godless Hollywood types ("I thought we'd go out swinging tonight with some chicks!"). The battle begins to turn in their favor: "I can't believe it . . . you prayed to get rid of Dexter . . . and he's going out the door . . . that's really heavy!" Despite a minor setback ("Come on, Tim! He was born in a stable and died on a cross . . . do we have to go through this Jesus trip?"), they save their actor friend and get the director to admit that his film is based on the falsehood of evolution.

In a twist at the end, however, the director says, "I'm going to continue making evolution films."

The crusaders respond, "Even though it's brainwashing and damaging these kids . . . many will lose their souls because of these films."

"I know!" the man says.

"Then what in Heaven's name would possess you to do such a thing?"

"You gentlemen serve your god . . . and I in turn will serve mine . . . his name is 'money' . . . and I need all I can get!"

My mom, thin and athletic-looking, was a chowhound and especially loved a free meal, and while she must have known what Shirl's offer was about, she probably figured that all they wanted was her time. She had nothing but time, so who was outfoxing whom?

The comic ended with a call to action on the inside back cover. "THE BIG LIE IS BEING PUSHED WORLD WIDE IN THE UNIVERSITIES," it said. "NOW YOU MUST DECIDE . . . WHICH WAY WILL YOU GO?"

"What's on the menu?" my mom said.

Dinner—which came only after a series of announcements, introductions, opening prayers, pleas for money, pleas for membership, and more prayers— was chicken-fried something with lots of white gravy that smelled rich, like organ meat, and a ball of mashed potatoes smothered in more gravy that had slopped onto the green beans. Bullyboys in three-piece suits locked the only exits and stood in front of the doors with folded arms. A speaker got up to testify, then another, then a third, and as I finished my lemon bar, members of the audience began holding both their hands in the air.

I looked around curiously and wondered if Shirl and Hank had known this would happen. Shirl held her hands up in surrender and had her eyes closed so tightly it looked as if she was trying to imagine something. People around us began to speak in tongues, and a man a few seats down fell backward onto the floor and began thrashing, which gave a dozen others the same idea. Someone up front was being cured of cancer by being shouted at, and the sound system squealed with feedback. The sick woman was held up by two men, and after the preacher gave her a rabbit-punch to the solar plexus, they let her fall writhing to the floor. Thank you, Jesus!

Even in the incredible din of that long banquet room, where I imagined the SIU Biology Club might hold its awards dinners, I could hear louder noises—people bellowing angrily in the hallway and pounding on the outside of the doors with their fists, demanding to come in. The scared looks of the bullyboys scared me more than I already was. Maybe it was the Devil, I thought. One of the guards made the mistake of opening a door just a crack to see what was going on, and I caught a glimpse of a dozen transvestites in lots of makeup. There was a small scuffle with cursing on both sides, and the bullyboys determinedly slapped hands out of the way and slammed the door again.

A couple of hours later the dinner was over, and we were finally allowed to leave. My mom said to Shirl and Hank, "Oo-wee, that was something *else*. Thanks a *lot*." But everyone hugged and said goodbye, and she and I walked out through the student center. It was quiet, but I was up so far past my bedtime that lateness rang in my ears, and I shivered with fatigue. I loved SIU's campus and had always equated it with my imagined adventures of adulthood—learning things from college professors and becoming, oh, a photojournalist. And a forest ranger. I felt a little dazed and wondered how this place of reason, truth, and academic discourse had sustained the visitation I'd just witnessed.

My mom and I glanced at each other at the same moment, and she grinned a little and shook her head. I felt very close to her. We had survived something true together and come out with humor intact.

The truth of the cream gravy came back to me repeatedly on the walk to the car. It was a summer's night before widespread air-conditioning. Stars spun in the sky; the crickets and cicadas sang madly. We rode home in our little white Toyota station wagon, away from Carbondale, past murky Crab Orchard Lake like a hole in the dark and the National Wildlife Refuge, which hid munitions dumps from the war and a federal prison. Cool humid air rushed in the front windows and out the back. I lay my head on her lap and fell asleep as only a child can, lulled by rocking and the glow from the radio dial, his mother steering him safely home through the dangers of the world.

Being Mistaken for Bookish

Of course I am bookish, proudly, and will be even more bookish when I finish training our dogs, Leo and Sonya Tolstoy, to be competent babysitters. But I'm also a man of action, and the injustice of being presumed merely bookish, simply because I teach English and write, is so maddening that it makes me want to run straight to the library to console myself.

We've always encouraged Starbuck to try different sports, giving him opportunities I didn't have. That summer he'd started his second season of T-ball. Some of the dads helped out. One of them, a friend, went to college on a baseball scholarship. Another, when he wasn't teaching the kids something, stood throwing the ball fifty feet in the air and catching it in the glove behind his back without looking. There were four or five of these guys, plus the coach, and they all fired balls at each other from outfield to home to third base, raising small explosions of dust from their well-worn mitts.

One afternoon, sitting with the sideline moms, I was hurting. I'd rented a chainsaw and taken down a tree on our property, straining things already bent back in a game of Here Chum de Bad Guys with two-year-old Wolfie. Truth was, I could barely walk, so I sat there reeking of two-cycle smoke and chain oil, covered in sawdust, ruined, wrecked. I kept thinking, "My first heart attack is coming . . . now . . . *now* . . . here it is, NOW." But the other dads didn't know any of that, and their odd looks made me glower at being judged. Stupid boring practice: it went on forever, then past forever because the dads were having so much fun they let the kids bat another round. Stupid fun.

I was raised by women. They weren't women who enjoyed a good Friday-night football game. My mom was athletic, but her choice of sports reflected her class notions, love of nature, and need for solitude. As an undergrad at her private college she fenced and played tennis; later she developed some vaguely continental or British idea that a brisk hike up and down hills on a cold rainy day built character. She and I spent a lot of time outdoors, joined the Sierra Club, and went on more than one *volksmarch*. She hated team sports such as baseball and football, associating them with machismo, anti-intellectualism, and aggression—even the domestic violence she'd experienced.

More than anything, I think she pitied the male of the species for keeping himself in thrall to his various balls.

When I was old enough for Little League she told me she'd come to every game if I wanted to play, but I saw right through her. She was happy when I chose to spend my time hiking, camping, and riding quarter horses on trails through the strip mines, and I was happier still climbing high up tall trees to watch the neighbor woman sunbathe. I had the kind of vanishing Huck Finn boyhood where I escaped members of the rival gang by knowing to smash backward into a honeysuckle bush in the forest, stop the cracking of wicker, and calm my breath as the bad guys searched in vain.

I can canoe, kayak, rappel, hump long distances with heavy things strapped to my back, read a map and compass, and identify plants and animals. I used to run and play tennis and guerilla soccer. I build things with dangerous power tools, know some demolitions and weapons. I was an army frogman, for god's sake. I can even swaddle the hell out of an infant. Haven't I proved my manhood?

Nope. I'm a shameful freak, positively un-American. It doesn't matter that some dads can't swim and sourly watch me porpoising with the kids at birthday parties at the aquatic center. What's important is that I can't tell you how many people are on any sort of team, from baseball to hockey. Do they even play hockey for real, or is it all like the Hanson Brothers in the movie *Slap Shot*? I don't own a glove, bat, stick, helmet, pads, cup, or a single item of clothing with a sports logo.

It must be marvelous to sit with your sons on a summer afternoon in the confines of Wrigley, dogs and Cokes in your hands, brimming with stats about your home team, the St. Louis Browns, and telling the boys who they'll see in the tenth quarter of the match with the Brooklyn Eckfords. I know how important all this is to American manhood, because I always weep when Kevin Costner's ghost-dad comes out of the corn to play catch with his middle-aged son in *Field of Dreams*.

I want to be part of the team, if only so my sons don't remember me as the weird, bullet-headed dad sitting alone in a half-sized lawn chair at their games. I want to learn. At the end of Starbuck's practice I listened with interest as the coach explained to the children the most basic rules of play: "This is second base. You run to it from first base."

I waved my hand eagerly and called, "Ooh, coach! Then you run to third?"

I could tell by how the other dads looked at me that I was in. All I needed to do by Tuesday was read a book on how to catch.

Notes for an Essay on Race and Class in a University Town

I'll call him Johnny Massacre, but his real name was more violent.

He welcomed us to the neighborhood a decade ago. It was the only welcome we got, other than the neighbors on one side. He said the previous owner of our house had employed him as a handyman, so he knew all about it if we needed him to tell us. He waved cheerily at my family and friends and asked if he could help them carry boxes in from the moving van, and I said no thanks, and he said well you'll need those magnolia petals raked up from the sidewalk 'cause they get slick as shit when they rot and you wouldn't want somebody to slip on 'em and anyway later they gonna stink like fourteen motherfuckers, a word he slurred into two syllables. You got a rake? I'll take care of them right now and you can pay me what you think is fair.

Johnny Massacre was younger than me but looked older. He was missing his front teeth and had a scar on his face. He had hard, lean muscles, and the tops of his ears looked tightly pinned to his head, like he'd been a fighter. He often grew a short afro, which he swept straight back, and a thin goatee and moustache. His pants were always a little too big, cinched tight with a belt, and more often than not he wore a nice button-down shirt or a striped polo, under a hoodie jacket, and cheap but functional shoes. He had large, expressive eyes and sometimes wore glasses that made him look scholarly or like a revolutionary. Other times his eyes were squinched narrow and bloodshot as hell.

Johnny Massacre was a very hard worker, I saw, after I hired him the first time to rake leaves. A true capitalist, he always bid the job ridiculously low to make his labor attractive then worked as fast as he could to maximize profits. He also never finished the job as agreed and held its completion hostage. After a while I knew this was part of the terms of his employment and waited for him to ring the doorbell so the second round of negotiations could begin. He'd excitedly tell me he could pull the weeds growing in the ivy at the side of my house and would go into great detail about how he'd do it. After he'd had his say, I'd point out he hadn't yet raked all the leaves we'd already discussed. He'd counter by saying he'd finish that up, plus pull the weeds, and all for just another twenty bucks, which made it sound like he was doing me a favor. I often agreed since the sum was reasonable even when I threw in a sandwich, chips, fruit, and a bottle of beer without being asked. He never left without making me consider future work, and he rarely came back to do it as promised.

I asked if he knew who laid the brick sidewalk along my house, and he said naw, man. I asked if he knew how long the enormous elm in my backyard had been threatening to split, and he said naw, man. I asked if the guy who owned the house before me ever paid him to work in the yard, and Johnny said naw, and I said but I thought you told me he did, and he said most of the white muhfuher in this neighborhood are afraid of a black man, you know what I'm saying? You're the only one who'll come to the door and talk to me.

Population figures ran as high as 210,000, but that was for both twin cities and probably the surrounding area and the transient student population too. We had America's fourteenth-largest campus, the second-largest food manufacturing plant in the world, one decent and one defunct indoor mall, countless strip malls, and recent additions of Starbucks, Potbelly Sandwich Works, Cold Stone Creamery, and other businesses well above Hardee's / IHOP / Arby's in the food chain. People often thought of it as a small town in the corn belt, but we had the crime of a medium-sized city and a very obvious gap between rich and poor, which often meant white and black. On the busy road north to the big box stores, kids from the lower-income neighborhood walked across five lanes of traffic nonchalantly, slowly, fatalistically, as if daring suv drivers to take anything else from them. The most recent spike in campus crime had been "sport" beatings of white male students by two or more black men, who were never students.

Don't like to be told there's huge disparity between rich and poor in America? Four hundred families hold half of all the wealth in this country. How you like that, muhfuher?

Many university employees owned houses in a small area of town known as "the faculty ghetto," a weirdly inverted nickname for privilege. When my wife and I mentioned to other parents that our house was on the fringe of this area, qualifying our children to go to the best public elementary school, they sighed, Ohh, as if we had no worries, but they chose to buy plywood McMansions on the outskirts of town with the other professionals and businesspeople, in neighborhoods designed to be so insular they might as well have been gated.

Our street led down from a struggling business district that was only about three blocks long and had a methadone clinic, county courthouse, and jail. Semis and beer trucks used the street as a shortcut to get to the highway. Student apartment buildings, a mechanic's garage, a liquor store, a health-food store, and a park district office mixed with Victorian houses in what some were trying to legislate a historical district. The gutters on our own house, which was on the National Historic Register, were rusting through, and we badly need a new roof, but the enormous elm would have to come down first, a job bid at several thousand dollars. We had no money for any of that.

With no place of his own, Johnny said he stayed up with his girlfriend in that house on the corner, half a block away, on Boneyard Creek. The house had been converted to apartments, and there was a Hispanic guy who lived there who walked past our house every morning to his food-service job, and a young white couple with a cat that they walked outside on a leash. The lot next door to the apartments used to have an empty Victorian house on it. I was told the fire was started by homeless addicts. After it burned to the walls it was razed by the owner, a hardworking landlord who'd rather knock down his older properties anyway and build new apartments, for college students.

Johnny's girlfriend was an obese white woman he'd yell at as they walked down the other side of the street. Once I waved to them and he left her standing there to come talk to me. For some reason he denied, that time, she was his girlfriend. I saw him daily outside her place, tending a smoking barbecue grill, listening to music or the news, drinking a tallboy. Every year he planted a couple of tomato plants and some flowers by her back door. He often had parties in the gravel driveway for his own friends.

He'd see me, from his rocking chair next to the driveway, walking my kids home from school and always yelled, "Pops!" in delight, his hand raised high, like a child waiting to be called on in class.

He said his Moms lived across town and that he sometimes stayed with her. She made great cream cakes, he said, and described them so insistently and in such delicious detail that I offered to buy one for our holiday table. He said, I'll set you up with some of that shit, Pops!, they're good, man, I swear, my Moms will make one for you. Of course I never got one.

One time my kids and I walked past when Johnny was standing in his yard with two teen girls. He introduced one as his niece. You won't understand when I say he affectionately cussed her viciously, telling her to stay put while he walked with me to ask about work. She grinned and teased him by following us, and he threatened, lovingly, to kick her fuckin' dumb little bitch ass all the way back up to his girlfriend's apartment. And you best be using your head to stay safe, he added, when you're surfing that web up there.

Johnny Massacre had a MySpace page, which I only found later. He had three friends, including the fake administrator that MySpace assigns as everyone's first friend. Johnny wrote, as the title of his MySpace page, a caption intended for his photo: "Johnny Playing with my PUSSY! [I mean CAT!] LOL Love my sadie!"

My mother-in-law and I sometimes discussed how, in the towns where we grew up, the homeless and mentally ill were known by everyone and, in an odd way, often protected and respected as something central to the town's identity. In Inner Station, the homeless were more transient, except for Grizzly Adams, an old white guy who kept his bags in the doorway of the city building, and The Cowboy, a black man in cowboy hat and boots who sat on sidewalks in campus town. The Cowboy had died recently.

Johnny Massacre was an ex-con. I found this out, after I knew him a year or two, by googling him, and the state's felons list popped up. The link is broken now, but as I remember it, he'd committed a nonviolent crime compounded by a failure to appear.

In ten years I never asked him once to come inside my house. It occurred to me that if I angered him he might burglarize it or, worse, break and enter when my children were inside. I sometimes looked at him closely, sizing him up.

Yet there's an odd comfort in being on friendly terms with a former criminal. What do I mean by that? I'm not sure.

After growing up in a small working-class town and doing time in army units that were 40 percent black, I still had some dual speech when I wanted. Johnny heard this early on and seemed to relax. He had a hilarious, loud, raspy voice and was full of energy and life. My wife and kids would be steps away, and he'd be yelling muhfuher this and that and grabbing his balls and dick and laughing kk-kkk-kk in the back of his throat.

Johnny Massacre rang the doorbell and handed me a plastic grocery bag. Inside was some half-thawed, freezer-burned meat that was already unwrapped. I knew I wouldn't serve it, and if I took it he'd use it as an excuse to ask for favors later. I said we didn't really eat beef ribs, so thanks but no. His look of disdain and shock at something so stupid: Who has the choice of what to eat?

He always rode a ten-speed or was on foot. Two or three times I saw him walking near the town library, talking to himself loudly, his eyes angry and wild.

Johnny Massacre cussed my wife's mother, who was nearly eighty. That sounds bad, but she was tough, maybe the hardest-working woman I've known, and had been in the Royal Navy. She grimaced when she pulled up that day and I told her Johnny Massacre was coming to work but that all she'd need to do was hand him his money, since I'd be on campus. When he did two-thirds of the work, knocked on the door and demanded the money, she told him he'd have to finish the job. He stomped around cussing her, acting like it was under his breath, but he finished the job.

He and his girlfriend tried to get me to participate in a food stamps scam. I was to pay them cash, something less than the value of the debit card, and the girlfriend and Mrs. Churm would go buy groceries for us with the card. When I refused, Johnny was insistent, then angry, then desperately insistent. Another time he asked me to buy two large sacks filled with basic food staples he got free from the food pantry at the Catholic church down the street.

I took Johnny with me to pick up more lawn bags because he said his favorite smoke shop was next door to the Walgreens, and he could use some blunts. I bought the blunts. In the confined space of the family car, he hacked and coughed and spit into tissues nonstop. At my routine physical I asked my doctor if I could catch TB from ten minutes with him.

A few days after President Obama was elected, Johnny Massacre came to work for me. I had to run out and asked if I could bring him something from McDonald's. He asked to ride along. When I brought up the election and said it was about time we had a black man in the White House, he shut up and didn't speak again, not once. His eyes glittered psychotically, and it was the one time I thought he might attack me. Even after I had bought his lunch in the drive-through and we returned to my house, he quivered with rage.

Johnny often showed up to ask for a dollar or two, his breath smelling like beer or liquor. He started ringing the bell after the kids were in bed. Also, my porch light burned out a lot, and all I could see going to the door was a dark figure through the glass. Picture his long sly talk in buildup to asking for a handout for smokes, and my exasperation standing with him in the cold darkness or the humid dark whining with mosquitoes.

There were times, when he was sober and it was daylight, that I wished I could do more for him. But what could it have been? He asked once if I would be a reference, and I said yes, but he pulled out an official form and asked me to write down that I was a nonprofit employer and to lie about the number of hours he'd worked so he'd be entitled to benefits. He was angry when I refused, and I was irritated with him.

Ever get hassled by a homeless guy in the city when you don't have money to buy your own lunch, let alone send your kids to the park district educational camps where all their friends will be? And you know when he looks at you he sees credit and a place to live and store your stuff, and he's right?

I sometimes gifted Johnny Massacre the flavored beers I didn't like from multipacks: the Cranberry Lambic, the Scotch Ale, the Harvest Pumpkin Ale, the overhopped Noble Pils. Once after I hadn't seen him in a while he said he'd been arrested on his bike for carrying an open container—which I had given him, he told me with a look of cunning.

Johnny Massacre reminded me a little of Thoreau.

Sometimes I had to tell him why his ideas for helping me fix up the place were a little ill-advised. I didn't need a water garden, for instance. Dousing my side yard in kerosene and setting it ablaze might not be the best way to clear weeds when the neighbor's house was a dozen feet away. And if he tore out my front porch to rebuild it from the ground up in the way he described, its roof would collapse. I shut him down on practically every-thing he proposed. When I relented for normal work he very often never showed up, and I had to change my plans in order to do it myself. In that way time passes quickly, and I often lost track of when I had last seen him.

It was terribly, unusually cold that winter.

At some point, maybe Thanksgiving week, he rang the bell and handed me a bottle of red wine he said he'd bought special for me for thirty bucks. I don't know wine and was afraid he might have spent the money, so I looked it up online. As with most things, opinions of it varied:

"[The wine] started out a bit tight with earthy flavors that went well with a sharp cheddar cheese and as the night went on it opened to release more fruit and chocolate flavors. Finish was short and light. A nice wine but many others out there at a better price point for the same quality."

"Plonk. Cheap. Alcoholic. Unmemorable."

I still have that undrunk bottle.

Johnny Massacre died the week before Christmas at the hospital where my sons were born, two blocks from my house. I didn't know until the third week of January and then only because I googled him again for some reason. Maybe I had a feeling he was in prison again and wondered if I'd dodged a bullet. I still don't know how or why he died. Neither the funeral home nor the police answered my e-mail queries, and no one else I knew had anything to do with him. I shouted out, Who killed Johnny Massacre? when after all it was you and me.

A friend who always thought I acted like some kind of liberal soft touch asked, You didn't hear him knocking on your window one cold night, saying, Let me in, did you?

The local paper ran an obituary of 161 words. Johnny was forty-three and preceded in death by his father, Johnny Massacre Jr. He was survived by his mom, three brothers (including another Johnny), three sisters, and two step-sisters. He was born in Chicago but graduated from a high school in our town, where he ran track. The piece described him as a very reliable handyman, very funny, and loyal, and a fisherman—in his spare time.

At an online site called *Tributes*, there were only two lines about his life. Then: "*Tributes* received this obituary from the Social Security Death Index, a public source. No further information other than what is displayed is available." In the cold, partial knowing of the Internet, he was still listed as alive on *MyLife* and *Reunion.com*. An uncle of mine was there too, 105 years old. He died in the 1970s.

Every school day I walked my sons home and felt an instant of tiny dread as we approached his girlfriend's house, thinking Johnny would be outside and would collar me to insist on work. He'd take my time, and nothing much would come of it. But, oh, that's right—his empty rocker in the front yard, and unplanted tomato patch—I remember.

The fact that I am writing about him, and not the other way around, is significant too.

Looking for Writers Beyond Their Work

America's personality was once riverine, and all roads led to the wharf. Mark Twain writes, "When I was a boy, there was but one permanent ambition among my comrades in our village on the west bank of the Mississippi River. That was, to be a steamboatman."

But rivers no longer occupy the same place in our national consciousness, and towns like Hannibal, Missouri, where in the mid-1800s up to a thousand boats landed every year, were cut off like oxbow meanders when railroads, interstates, and then airplanes came along.

No boats were expected in Hannibal on April 21, 2010—one hundred years to the day after Mark Twain's death—or for the rest of eternity, near as I could tell. Even the resident *Mark Twain Riverboat*, a 120-foot stern-wheeler built in 1964, sat idle and dark. Two policemen walked quickly through the narrow waterfront park, glancing over at someone shouting in the distance. Soon the shouting man and I were the only people on the bank as far as I could see in either direction.

He was fishing below a work barge tied off to some mutilated sheet-piling. He loaded up a giant hook with glop that I took for peanut butter but may have been his secret-formula catfish bait, and swung the rod hard and fast. The bait went flying off the hook and splashed down separately at a distance. He shouted an obscenity, reeled in, scooped up two fingers more of the glop from its jar, formed it carefully around the hook, and cast again with the same result. More savage cussing, more bait, another cast, same results.

I stood next to him companionably as the obscenities rained down, their thunder rolling across the Mississippi all the way to Jackson Island. Others might have felt uncomfortable in the situation, but you see I've *gone* fishing myself, once. Twain wrote in his notebook in 1898, "If I cannot swear in heaven I shall not stay there," and for a split second I wondered if it was *him*.

~~~

Why do we go looking for writers beyond their work? They are, after all, *unpleasant* people.

I know, for instance, a writer who was mixed up in a university phone-sex scandal; a writer who still can't drink *Cuba libres* because it makes him want the cocaine he used to do when he drank them with Mongolian prostitutes; a writer who replies to greetings with farts; a writer whose pedagogy involves giving students vile nicknames; and a writer who used to eat dirt.

And that's just Facebook friends.

In the film *Amadeus*, the composer Salieri sneaks into the room where Mozart writes. Salieri lifts Mozart's pen from its pot of ink and stares quizzically at it, as if it might provide a clue to how, in Salieri's words, "music, finished as no music is ever finished," "the very voice of God," came from "that giggling, dirty-minded creature I had just seen crawling on the floor!"

This perfectly dramatizes our puzzlement over the gap between art and artist.

~~~

The centenary of Twain's death was also the 175th anniversary of his birth, and the 125th anniversary of *Huck Finn*. I drove out to Hannibal to catch the ceremony at his boyhood home, where a time capsule would be buried in the presence of a Mark Twain impersonator, a beauty queen, and a dozen Tom Sawyer and Becky Thatcher "ambassadors" dressed in hokum-wear. I knew Twain would have enjoyed the ceremony, if only for the chance to soundly cuss so many so efficiently.

The interstate west of Springfield, Illinois, quickly narrows to an old state road ribboned with tar. In spring the bare soil across much of Illinois is monochromatic because it's been tilled uniformly by computer-controlled machines in fields that extend flatly to the horizon. But just west of the capital, the first low hills emerge, and the plowed dirt begins to look less corporate.

Trees grew along the route, the tender mist of their leaves punctuated with redbud blooms, and marsh weed and cattails grew in the ditches. None of this was allowed to exist along major highways in the east-central part of the state, where I lived, and seeing it made me happy. Drainage creeks twisted through the fields in tight green serpentines, miniatures of the lower river on which Twain piloted as a young man. The sunlight changed too, so inexplicably that it's tempting to refer to old theories about miasmal exhalations of the earth.

A sign marked 90 degrees west longitude: "¼ way west around the world." Exits led to the hometowns of Stephen Douglas, John Hay, and John Nicolay. Lincoln was clerking at New Salem, Illinois, thirty miles from Hannibal, when Sam Clemens was a toddler cutting teeth. Grant worked in St. Louis and upstream at Galena, and General John Logan was born three hours south, near my hometown. I stopped at a Dairy Queen in this cradle of the American Civil War and bought the best chargrilled burger with cheese food and crunchy tomatoes I'd ever had.

Closer to the river, road-cuts exposed sandstone and limestone, and the highway crossed a long floodplain surrounded by distant bluffs. I experienced a microsecond of confusion. The landscape stood before me, irreconcilable with Twain's prose and my own memories, yet irrefutable. At least crossing the Mark Twain Memorial Bridge was no longer the terror it was when I was a kid and my mom wrestled the steering wheel of her little car, its tires pulling and shimmying, on the deck plates of previous bridges, while I looked far, far down at the boiling brown god.

On the Missouri embankment there was a fifty-foot high portrait of Twain in the medium of colored gravel. The road twisted around a hill and down past gas stations and a tanning salon into the center of Hannibal, where a trim business district contained the Mark Twain Dinette, Mark Twain Family Restaurant, Twain Tours with Twainland Express, Mark Twain Book and Gift Shop, Mrs. Clemens' Shoppes, and Pudd'nhead's Antiques, Collectibles and Crafts.

Twain's boyhood home was there too, a small clapboard house that looked taller than it was wide, with other period or reconstructed buildings in a block's radius: a reconstructed version of the Blankenship home (the boy was a model for Huck Finn), a period building being called the Becky Thatcher House, the drugstore building where the Clemenses lived for a while, and the courtroom where Twain's dad was a justice of the peace. Two blocks away on Cardiff Hill, where Twain played pirate as a boy and real bootleggers and other criminals lived, the town had installed a statue of Tom and Huck, a small butterfly garden up the slope, and a lighthouse on top, used not for navigation but to honor Twain.

The ceremony turned out to be respectful and sedate, mostly citizens of Hannibal gathering to honor one of their own, with few tourists and no broadcast media. Even the Earthcam pointed at the front door of Twain's home wasn't working.

The Twain impersonator took the microphone and did two or three well-chosen bits from Twain's repertoire. He invoked Twain's line, "Let us endeavor so to live that when we come to die even the undertaker will be sorry," which was poignant after he'd read the *Hannibal Courier-Post*'s obituary for Twain, published the morning after his death. The child ambassadors described what they had learned as Toms and Beckys, and one little girl spoke movingly about becoming president and alleviating the misery of the poor. I had only to turn my head and look up the steep incline of Hill Street to see the mix of dilapidated and well-kept houses that reflected the widening disparity in America, worse perhaps than in Twain's Gilded Age. Proclamations were read aloud from the governor, the U.S. congresswoman for the district, and the mayor; 2010 was proclaimed the Year of Mark Twain in Hannibal, Missour-*uh*. After the ceremony, people drifted back to their workplaces and into restaurants.

Feeling sad, I took a photo of a horse wearing a hat. Then I walked through the park to the river landing and along the decline of the wharf, the cobblestones so worn their edges stuck up like stone knives. I tried to cast myself back to 1853, when Twain left home, but two steel trestle bridges spanned the river now, railroad tracks paralleled the wharf with a levee beyond them, and there were masses of overhead wires, satellite dishes, and advertising signs.

Yet the river was utterly placid and smoothly flowing, even glassy, and purling the only hint at the mischief of which it was capable. Hannibal boomed after Twain left, then the boom days ended, and now Glascock's Landing felt very close again in *spirit* to how Twain described his town in *Life on the Mississippi*:

> After all these years I can picture that old time to myself now, just as it was then: the white town drowsing in the sunshine of a summer's morning; the streets empty, or pretty nearly so; one or two clerks sitting in front of the Water Street stores, with their splint-bottomed chairs tilted back against the wall, chins on breasts, hats slouched over their faces, asleep—with shingle-shavings enough around to show what broke them down; a sow and a litter of pigs loafing along the sidewalk, doing a good business in watermelon rinds and seeds; two or three lonely little freight piles scattered about the "levee"; a pile of "skids" on the slope of the stone-paved wharf, and the fragrant town drunkard asleep in the shadow of them; two or three wood flats at the head of the wharf, but nobody to listen to the peaceful lapping of the wavelets against them; the great Mississippi, the majestic, the magnificent Mississippi, rolling its mile-wide tide along, shining in the sun; the dense forest away on the other side; the "point" above the town, and the "point" below, bounding the river-glimpse and turning it into a sort of sea, and withal a very still and brilliant and lonely one.

Twain returned five times as an adult. From his notebook of April 1882: "Alas! Everything has changed in Hannibal—but when I reached Third or Fourth Street the tears burst forth, for I recognized the mud. It at least was the same—the same old mud."

The mud of Hannibal has been largely paved over but still rises in the brick of the buildings sprawled over the hills. It's a decent metaphor for how great writers become part of the edifice of a nation, though Twain had doubts about what portion of him would remain.

"We struggle, we rise," he writes, "with the adoring eyes of the nations upon us, then the lights go out . . . our glory fades and vanishes, a few generations drift by, and naught remains but a mystery and a name."

"Fuck!" the disgruntled fisherman yelled over my shoulder.

In his essay "Writer and Region," Wendell Berry says: "There is something miraculous about [Huck Finn's voice]. It is not Mark Twain's voice. It is the voice, we can only say, of a great genius named Huckleberry Finn, who inhabited a somewhat lesser genius named Mark Twain, who inhabited a frustrated businessman named Samuel Clemens."

This phenomenon is made possible by a technology—black squiggles on white paper—that stores ideas and verbal images so we can see and manipulate them over time by the process of revision. What we love in a writer is this *recursive* voice, the most concentrated form of that person's best awareness, which can be kept in print, shelved in libraries, and stored in a digital cloud that smiles down from heaven. At its best it's like having a sane, just, brilliant friend who can never die.

But the distilled intensity and sometimes near-perfection of recursive work also explains, I think, the deflation we sometimes feel meeting artists. The *work* has been shaped over time with the aid of a thousand self-critics; the person who *wrote* it crunches dill pickles in his maw while talking to you on the phone.

The final disconnect is that, unlike its art, the human animal is mortal. Your friend's work may have encouraged you to see and feel, but he or she is always waving goodbye from the fantail of a departing ship.

"Even Beatles die," writes poet Valzhyna Mort.

I can't reconcile that.

〜〜〜

Too often, so-called American innocence—in politics, religion, science—is no different from cynicism. Twain's great gift was to find a way to reconcile knowledge and innocence, what Picasso meant when he said, "It takes a lifetime to become young."

It's not fashionable to speak of greatness of spirit, so let's say Twain was an innocence broker and that that quality in his work hypnotizes us, like birds before a snake. I refer of course to the child narrators, the attention to "innocents" staggering abroad (his best-seller in his lifetime), the prose that has us believing *he's* normal but surrounded by odd and colorful characters, the personas of the naïf and the put-upon victim, the spotless white ice-cream suits, the image of the loving family man performing skits at home with his beloved children.

Call Twain avuncular if you like, but he put these qualities to work battling imperialism, racism, vivisection, cant, hypocrisy, sham, and injustice. He could also be viciously angry, cornpone, and hilariously filthy. Lecturing at a Stomach Club dinner on the topic of masturbation he reputedly said, "A jerk in the hand is worth two in the bush." By becoming in his work a whole human being, he shows how to love our muddy experience and gives us hope that *people* can be whole too.

~~~

One of the dangers of confusing the writing and the life is that the author's stuff becomes as suffused with meaning as his books. The Mark Twain Museum, separate from the boyhood home, is modern, cheerfully lighted, and contains an incoherent mishmash of objects that's still interesting and even moving: the death mask of Twain's only son, a little boy shown in a photo sitting up in his stroller; items of Twain's clothing; a pipe with the stem worn away by his teeth; two dozen paintings and sketches by Norman Rockwell for an edition of *Tom Sawyer*; a reproduction pilot's wheel; furniture from various households; and period newspapers.

The front page of the *Hannibal Morning Journal*, Friday, April 22, 1910, says Clemens was "bad in the morning at Stormfield" (his last home, near Redding, Connecticut) but "seemed in good spirits" and recognized his wife's nephew and niece.

> Unable to talk too much, he asked the nurse for his glasses. When he was given them he picked up a book which for many years had been one of his favorites, Carlyle's *French Revolution*, and read several pages of it. This exertion was too much for his fast-failing strength, and he relapsed into a comatose condition, which verged into complete unconsciousness from which he never recovered.

It's fitting that a display in the museum quotes a passage from *Innocents Abroad*, in which Twain complains about the ubiquity of holy relics in his travels in Europe and the Middle East:

But isn't this relic matter a little overdone? We find a piece of the true cross in every old church we go into, and some of the nails that held it together. I would not like to be positive, but I think we have seen as much as a keg of these nails.

There are other kegs of Twain's nails on display a few blocks away at the other sites, and the gift shop at the boyhood home *sells* a few near-relics, should you want to take one home. In one corner I found Wild Huckleberry Gummi Bears, Wild Huckleberry Pancake Mix, Wild Huckleberry Cocoa, Wild Huckleberry Honey, Wild Huckleberry Syrup, Wild Huckleberry Chocolate Bar, Wild Huckleberry Jelly Beans, Wild Huckleberry Sampler, Wild Huckleberry Pinwheels, Wild Huckleberry Stix, Wild Huckleberry Taffy . . . and Missour-uh Chocolate River Rocks.

There were also books by and about Twain, steamboat models, jaw harps and pennywhistles, and all manner of other geedunk and geegaws. In response to my questioning, the two older southern ladies who staffed the cash register patiently explained that the huckleberries were not local but grown deep in the Ozarks. Of course I'd seen right through that, so I was pleased with myself when I found the jam to be delicious anyway, that my boys liked their T-shirts, and the postcards I bought of Twain, cartooned by *Calvin and Hobbes*'s Bill Watterson for the *Mark Twain Journal*, looked fine in my office. I began to plan another visit to pick up a few other things. Maybe a marble head.

We try to get *closer*. My friend Rory is rumored to have two bricks he took from the yard of William Faulkner's house, Rowan Oak. Rory's a big guy who lettered all the sports and for one afternoon flung cloth bags of flour for a living, but it's *rumored* there's a five-foot Faulkner scholar somewhere gonna kick his *ass*.

～～～

Sometimes it feels as if each of us is sunk in our own crystalline well. We think we know each other through the glass landscape until some event reveals how impossibly distant we are in that proximity, how another's singing was actually keening.

And yet. Once at a dinner I sat across from a poet and felt over the course of a short, broken conversation her enormous intelligence and consciousness focus on me. Such moments almost make the hard breaks of mortality bearable and drive us to search for more such experiences.

Then she walked out of the restaurant and kicked a dog. The dog was metaphorical.

〜〜

One of Twain's favorite words was "lonesome." He uses it eighteen times in the great moral novel *Huck Finn*. The novel *Tom Sawyer*, a boyhood fantasy by comparison, has only five mentions.

〜〜

There were many events celebrating Twain on the centenary, the biggest of them the release of volume 1 of his unexpurgated memoirs, which he insisted not be published until one hundred years after his death. Despite the book being a $35, four-pound, 500,000-word ramble, by Thanksgiving it had gone back to press six times, and the publisher still couldn't meet holiday demand. All this renewed interest made us feel closer to Twain, a presumption he would have appreciated, ham that he was, and been amused by.

As Twain prepared to leave Hannibal for the last time in his life, Tom Nash, a childhood friend—now deaf—approached him.

Twain writes: "[Nash] was old and white-headed, but the boy of fifteen was still visible in him. He came up to me, made a trumpet of his hands at my ear, nodded his head toward the [other] citizens [who'd gathered to say goodbye], and said, confidentially—in a yell like a fog horn—'Same damned fools, Sam.'"

Where Your Standardized Testing Money Goes

The Galt House Hotel in Louisville, Kentucky, bills itself as part of the "grand legacy of southern hospitality and excellence." The legacy part refers to the fact that Dickens stayed in the original Galt House in 1842, and Sherman and Grant "met here in March 1864 to plan the . . . 'March to the Sea.'" But that building burned down the next year. Another was built and was razed in 1921. This version was built in the Nixon era and would house a thousand of us in town to grade high school students' essays for the College Board's AP Exams. Our reading of them started on a Sunday and would last a week.

It was a pleasant drive down from Inner Station in my rented Dodge Something, which looked like it was built from leftover PT Cruisers. Clearly some designer thought it was pretty sexy, and mine was painted candy-apple red. I stepped hard on the accelerator to escape the glare of truckers, and the engine gave a mild growl like a housecat in heat.

I passed billboards along the way for Indiana's Biggest Joint Surgery Unit; a giant cafeteria with a Norman Rockwell collection; the nation's largest indoor RV showroom; and James Joyce's I-65 Truck Sales. The literary connection was a good omen, I thought. Fields of young corn the color of absinthe gave way to weedy floodplains, and I saw the bridges and high-rises of Louisville. The hotel was on the waterfront, and two paddle wheelers were docked below it.

Because housing was provided we had been assigned roommates, though I didn't know who mine would be, and he wasn't in the room when I checked in. It had been a while—a long while—since I had to share a room with a stranger, and of course I thought of Ishmael meeting his new roommate, Queequeg, who comes in late after selling embalmed human heads in the street. My own preference was for someone who was not just quiet, but *absent*. I'd signed up for seven more full days of grading after just finishing grading at the end of my own semester and was thinking maybe I should have gone to med school as I'd planned.

Buffet meals were also provided, and dinner that night was in an enormous space in the convention center. I sat at a table with three stats guys and two English lit women. The women had read before; one called this the "seven-day migraine." The other said it wasn't so bad but warned that the breaking point was day three. I laughed uncertainly.

The young stats guy from Minnesota, wanting badly to be positive, said to me, "You must like grading or you wouldn't be here."

I didn't mean to snap. "I like being paid *money* or I wouldn't be here," I said. He looked hurt.

Afterward I stopped in at Al J's Bar in the hotel. "I'm here for the AP grading!" customers announced before giving their drink orders, as if they were the VIPs the cocktail waitresses had been waiting for all week. The room looked out over the stacks of the steamboats to the big octagonal clock on the Colgate factory on the opposite bank. The bar counter was a thirty-foot long aquarium, maybe five inches deep, with a Plexiglas top to rest your drink on. I sat at the only open seat. Under my drink, one of the fish was dead and the other fish were pecking at its remaining eyeball.

"Ah cain't git it," the bartender told me. "Hon, ah cain't fahnd mah fish net."

I put my cocktail napkin over the scene, but there were some pretty big koi that kept dragging the corpse around so I was forced to look. I finished up my beer and left. Is it the fate of all parents of young children to start wishing they were home as soon as they've made their long-anticipated escape?

I took a walk along the riverbank and up to the burgeoning Fourth Street Live area, a block of restaurants and bars with open street-drinking and live music. I walked as long as I could before I returned to my room, where I sat on my bed, reading the essay questions and reviewing other materials

Educational Testing Services (ETS) had provided, until I heard the latch slide back as someone put his card in the door, and my roommate—normal, smart, a private high-school teacher from Massachusetts, a family man, a Yalie, and a Whiffenpoof—came in and introduced himself. To my relief, Peter was no cannibal. He wasn't even an Americanist. And given this was bourbon country, I thought we might be able to work out an accord.

～～

Jim Barkus, chief reader for AP literature, told us our punctuality each day and steady application to the task would get the job done by Saturday evening: we weren't to worry about our speed. It was a little hard not to think of speed, though. The scale of the production was staggering.

According to the College Board, there were nine thousand college faculty and AP teachers "from around the world" grading ("reading") the eight million essays written for 2.3 million AP exams taken in twenty-two subject areas in May 2007. By the end of that summer, readers would have gathered at the College of New Jersey, Colorado State University, the Ocean Center in Daytona Beach, Trinity University in Texas, the University of Nebraska, and there in Louisville.

Our share was some nine hundred thousand essays/problems in English literature, French, and statistics. Two years earlier, Barkus said, there were forty thousand fewer exams read at this location, so they had tried to staff appropriately. Unfortunately, seventy-five readers had failed to show, so he asked us to work an extra half-hour each day until ETS could be assured we'd finish.

Essays were read holistically, based on an evaluative rubric with a ten-point scale, and there were constant efforts to keep everyone normalized with their grading. Barkus said that "while [he was] distressed at the death of the apostrophe" (the crowd laughed; it was that sort of crowd), "students can get the highest score with a missed apostrophe." About 10 percent of essays were back-checked, read by pit bosses at each table, at least in the first three days. Barkus said we weren't to think of this as "Big Brother systematically checking our work, but after one hundred essays, the mind does slip."

Sixty percent of readers were recruited from colleges and universities (a mix of tenured faculty, adjuncts, and PhD candidates), and 40 percent from secondary ed. Only about 20 percent were new readers. Many had been readers for several years, and some had done it for decades. Barkus said that ETS was "very concerned" that 20–25 percent of readers should represent minorities, but that this reading "didn't quite yield 18 percent declared minorities."

The actual reading took place in what looked like the inside of an airport hangar in the Kentucky Convention Center in downtown Louisville. It was noisy and cold. One did not speak of the draft coming from the exposed ductwork fifty feet overhead; this was a *wind*, strong enough to move papers on the tables, and one of the six people around me was given a linen tablecloth to wear on his shoulders to get warm. A man at the next table of six readers said, "We're working inside the box that Disneyland came in."

Readers in English lit were assigned one of three questions that students had faced the month before. Those reading question 1 spent the week reading compare/contrasts of two poems by Richard Wilbur and Billy Collins. Those with question 2 read about a relationship in Dalton Trumbo's *Johnny Got His Gun*. I was in the group for question 3, which asked students to write about how a character's relationship to the past manifests in a novel or play of their choosing. Nearly forty titles had been suggested, from *Ethan Frome* to *Mrs. Dalloway* to *A Streetcar Named Desire*, but they could use others not listed. I'd say 20 percent of the essays I saw the first day were on *Great Expectations*, followed closely by *Great Gatsby* and *Beloved*.

Students had had two hours to handwrite the three essays, without books or revision to speak of, and some of the third essays written (question 3, if they went in order) looked rushed. Occasionally someone had doodled on the page that should have had an essay written on it or wrote cute things to us. Someone at my table had a story about a student who wrote, halfway through an essay, "I've been accepted at Harvard, and my boyfriend just proposed to me, so I don't feel like finishing this, but I want you to have a *nice day*."

At breaks there was a rush for the snack tables: apples, donuts, and mini-yogurt in the morning; popcorn, ice cream, and pretzel mix in the afternoon. The crush was terrible to see. ETS had made a decision not to provide bottomless urns of coffee in the room; it would only cause more frequent bathroom breaks and spills on student booklets. Needless to say, it's uncomfortable to sit all day on a folding chair, hunched over handwritten exam books, and management soon started us on mandatory four-minute stretching breaks. I'd love to have taken a picture of a thousand middle-aged teachers doing down-dog yoga poses, but my little camera wouldn't fit them all in the frame.

Midweek we neared the 50 percent graded mark. ETS said Saturday would be a full day, and that that was unusual.

All week our table leader went for meetings in the hallway every few hours. After one of these trips he revealed that he got fairly detailed statistics about our speed and performance as readers. (As we finished them, graded booklets with their bubble sheets were whisked away by an incredibly attentive crew of young people and were taken somewhere onsite to be run through an optical reader. Numbers were crunched nearly in real time.)

The good news he said was that our table was at least as fast as the room average, and we were slightly ahead in accuracy. I wondered what "accuracy" could mean in scientific terms, reading essays. He said the computer can predict essay scores based on the objective portion of the AP tests, a multiple-choice exam. Peter said it seemed unlikely that there would be a direct correlation, and I asked why ETS had students write essays at all, if it was possible to predict the scores accurately. The TL said there was a "0.4 correlation of objective to discursive sections," but he wasn't clear on what that meant. In any case, the statisticians at ETS had "millions of samples from many years of testing, so it's a deep well to draw from," he said. "Their job, after all, is to prove the validity of the tests."

Peter wondered if ETS had ever followed the college performance of students who had taken their tests. "That's creepy," I said. "But it would be interesting to see."

"It is a bit creepy," the table leader said. He looked disturbed.

He said he'd changed 25 percent of our scoring, a little or a lot, as he "back-checked" more than 10 percent of our exam books in the first days. He also knew that the room's average score on the essays was 4.88 points (out of 9 possible) and that our table was "reading slightly higher than that." He encouraged us to continue to "stick to the rubric, not to reward students." Since the stats showed we were accurate and ahead of the curve, it meant we'd just been given "good" folders (of twenty-five exam books each), so he cautioned that bad folders to come would look that much worse.

That afternoon, in the long slog to quitting time, I was so focused on a student paper that I used up the last of my attention and energy without realizing it and nearly fell off my chair. Many readers were standing, in order to stay awake and alert. It was a nasty little thrill to open to the back of the exam booklet and see nothing where question 3 should have been. Usually, though, it meant the student had written it first, so I flipped to the start to make sure. If it was there it meant the student had still had two hours of test time ahead of her when she wrote it, and lots and lots of nervous energy.

Here are some things I learned from student essays:

"In order to illustrate a general truth, an author will create a character, eliminating the need of an author to state his message. This helps teach a lesson to all its readers: We must accept each other for our successes and failures."

But: "Beauty has a price. Because of the beauty of the novel's protagonist, her past was filled with rape, loss of a child, loss of a husband, twice-over public scorn, hard labor, general mistreatment, all climaxing into an execution."

I was glad I hid my beauty deep, deep inside, where it belonged.

There are vocal critics to standardized testing in general, and the attempts to normalize the grading of so many readers, even on the same essay in practice sessions, reminded me of students' claims that "writing is subjective, so it can never be graded fairly." But my reaction to this enormous production was that the ETS brought in an army of the well qualified to judge, and while the mood was friendly, even light, these people were as serious as it was possible to be about getting it right for the students'—not the company's—sake.

Teachers everywhere like to share horror stories about students. It's a way of dealing with our anxiety over the difference between our ambitions for them (and thus for ourselves) and their actual comprehension and performance. The AP reading was no different. Probably a quarter of the talk at meals was about the silly things written in student essays. When I got home, a professor asked if I thought, having read all those essays, that students were getting worse.

I couldn't say, not having done this before and having a preconception that people are people and don't change easily. There were essays that looked to be written by the functionally illiterate; there were essays drowning in the inanity fostered by coaching, not teaching, and the mostly artificial limits of testing. But there were many, many essays that showed true understanding of notoriously difficult books and plays. Many others were written with verbal sensitivity, and some even had writerly grace.

Now and then someone would read aloud a portion of one of these essays, and the room of readers would groan in admiration. One student wrote an essay on *The Sound and the Fury* as a novel warning the South to relinquish its obsession with the past. The student quoted Faulkner in the essay, saying, "Clocks, or 'mausoleums of all human hope and desire,' are the subject of Quentin's hate and perpetual speculation. . . . Clocks tick the South's past grandeur away into the recesses of dusty memory."

Another chose to write about *Ulysses*, saying, "History is alive. . . . Joyce testifies that there is nothing new not only in this book but in the world; humans are rememberers, forgetters, recyclers, resemantifiers." And some damned kid wrote a response to the fishing scene in *Johnny Got His Gun*, which turned the falling pine needles into a symbol of the eternal that connected father, son, the earth, and all time; they read it in the big meeting on the last morning, and I sat blinking back tears. Then the week was over, mercifully, though I knew I'd miss sharing the experience of reading with the people I'd met. For a time it had felt . . . collegial.

~~~

On Saturday night I needed to get my own work done before I left for home the following morning, and I felt smugly valorous for doing it while everyone else was cutting loose to celebrate the end of our indenture. I had a couple of Maker's Marks in my room and decided to treat myself to a carryout steak and maybe some shrimp. Someone had said Joe's Crab Shack was popular and good, and it was close, so I strolled down the wharf with the setting sun on my back, feeling warm with accomplishment. There's something magical about a river town, even when it's selling itself, and even when signs on the wharf warn you not to eat anything you might pull out of the river, not to let the water touch your mucous membranes, not to look at the river threateningly, and not to think about it too hard if you're already feeling fragile. I stopped to look at the sign that listed famous writers who'd been there before, and it looked to me there might be room for my name at the bottom. It's not a long name.

At a curve in the path with no one else in sight, a man rose up to ask if I spoke Spanish. A little, I said. He ripped out some long sentences, and I said, Slower, please. The second time I got that his mom lived across the bridge, far across town, and there were difficulties. He needed money for the bus and for the difficulties. Between the bourbon and the accomplishment, I was feeling egalitarian and said although I had only two dollars in cash, he was welcome to one. I stupidly pulled out my wallet to show him. This amused him greatly. We talked, and he told me my Spanish was perfect. No, no, I demurred but launched into an explanation of being stationed in Panama a long time ago and, what a thing, I had been *un hombre rana*, a frog man, *un buceador*. . . .

He interrupted to ask if I liked to fish. I was still forming my reply, along the line of, "I prefer to swim underwater like fishes rather than catch them," when he pointed at the river and said something funny that depended on a colloquialism I didn't know. Somebody was a *cabrón*—who, I couldn't say. He roared with laughter and walked away waving my dollar bill in the air like a hanky.

Joe's was swarming with people, and the hostess told me to order my food at the bar. Every stool was taken, and people stood behind them, waiting to order. I stood there too, a long time, behind two bullet-headed young guys with construction tans and chipped teeth.

"You gotta put your money in plain view," one told me when he saw me straining to catch the bartender's eye. He had a twenty and a five on the bar in front of him.

They'd been drinking Joe's Ya-Yas, pint glasses full of vodka, peach schnapps, coconut rum, cranberry juice, pineapple juice, and grenadine. They asked for theirs with no ice. The drinks looked like watery Pepto-Bismol and left rings on the glass at each reduction, like dirty river foam. The first one told me he kept the straw from each drink so he knew how many he'd had. There were five straws upright in an empty glass, and he waved at the bartender, who came right away. I took the chance to order my steak.

He was a foreman on the Interstate 64 project going on noisily outside the restaurant, and he told me all the kinds of jackhammers he had up there. Many I had never heard of. He was due back on the job in a few hours, he said. But first, he and his buddy were going up to the Irish Festival on the waterfront to have some beers, and he guessed he'd probably do something dumb like tell a girl she was pretty in front of her boyfriend. They invited me to come along when they found out I was in town for the College Board reading, which they said they'd heard about.

When the first guy went to the toilet, his buddy told me how the stereotypes of Louisville and of Kentucky had it all wrong, from Dan'l Boone and the "coonskin cap crap" to bourbon, which was fine and good, but he liked a good Ya-Ya instead. He didn't know anybody who drank bourbon. Louisville was, simply, a great place to live. Real estate was affordable, and he ran down the advantages of the different neighborhoods for me. He told me the size of his house, and where he lived, and how much he paid for it, and why he hadn't been fit for the service even though he was an army brat. He was about to reveal something he wanted to say about his girlfriend when his buddy came back. They pounded two more Ya-Yas like morning orange juice and stood to leave.

"So think about it," the second said. I thought he wanted me to reconsider going to the Irish fest with them.

"Louisville really is a great place to live," he said, "and if you're thinking about buying a place here—even a second house, for a getaway—you should just do it."

~~~

The day I got home Mrs. Churm and I took the boys to the Inner Station library. In the kids' section I saw a PhD candidate I knew. He had a little girl Starbuck's age, and I saw him often in the library and the English Department. He never knew who I was, and when I forced the hello, he stared at me, reluctantly said hi, but refused to engage in conversation. Upstairs I met another young woman from the program, all in black with black cat-eyed glasses and black-dyed hair, who wouldn't even make eye contact. When we got home, a professor crept past our house in the enormous sunglasses she wore, even at night, so she didn't have to acknowledge other people.

The department hallways were full of them, faculty and grad students alike, the shuffling, the angry, the depressed, the morose, the morbidly jealous, the suspicious, the spiteful, the insecure—and for what? The hard labor of being intellectuals, which they willingly sentenced themselves to? They were not, after all, mucking out horse stalls for a living or cleaning squid or chipping concrete or going gray in cubicles somewhere. They weren't homeless.

"They'd bitch if they were being hung with a new rope," Frenchy said.

That night, back in my own bed, I dreamed of velvet ropes stretched across the door of a tenured professor's office. I couldn't tell if I was inside or out.

The Unlikelihood of Fathers

It was an improbable start to be born American in a French clinic in Saigon, Vietnam, on Ho Chi Minh's birthday, at the start of the Vietnam War. My mother said the Vietnamese nurses at my delivery giggled furiously.

My dad was on faculty at Southern Illinois University's Vocational Technical Institute, which at the start of the 1960s sent a team to Vietnam with the Agency for International Development, or USAID. In Saigon, he was assigned to Phu Tho National Institute of Technology and flew by four-person Pipers to towns in the Mekong Delta to help small industry.

Our family lived in a compound built, owned, and operated by the U.S. embassy. It was a neocolonial life. Diplomatic staff, foreign contractors, aid workers, and military families lived in spacious stilt-houses with big backyards. There was no rent. We had a maid who also cooked meals and cared for me, a gardener, and a driver we shared with other residents. My pigtailed sister kept a pet monkey and rode to school in a bus with grenade screens over the windows.

My mother was one of many foreigners in Saigon teaching English, the new language of ambition in the buildup, and she loved Vietnam and its people all her life. But the American War, as the Vietnamese called it, was growing, and her marriage was embattled. The November that both President Kennedy and South Vietnam's President Diem were murdered, we flew home as a family on leave. We were supposed to be going back when things settled down. But shortly after the flight landed in southern Illinois, my dad went one way and we went the other. Due to the war and subsequent embargo between both countries and spouses, for thirty years I would need more than a passport to see either Vietnam or my father again.

<center>~~~</center>

Boys who grow up fatherless ask endlessly, hopelessly, listlessly, "What is a father?", fearful of the answers, and unaware they're actually asking, "What does it mean to be a man?" For their troubles, they get castoff bits and dead pieces of fatherhood from other families and unchilded men, offered with the best intentions. The boys pat these together into golem-fathers that strut around grotesquely in war medals, clenching bubble pipes in their teeth and telling ridiculous tales.

When I was growing up, my father was little more than a Kodachrome ghost in a brown paper sack. On his first military ID, he looked like a young hell-raiser, crazy-intelligent-mean, if you wanted to see that. Maybe he *was* the Devil, as my mother said. But why then, in another photo, was the Devil an affable middle-aged man in a guayabera, sitting on a tropical lawn with a monkey on his back?

If you're a little devil yourself, you insist on knowing how these things go. When I was seven, they told us he'd been posted to Afghanistan, so I imagined him, oh, gazing up the Khyber Pass and drinking cups of tea. I couldn't imagine why he'd abandoned his infant son. When they said a few years later he'd moved to Indonesia, I searched books for the tin mines where he was said to advise.

Meanwhile I studied other fathers: a lawyer, a state trooper, engineers, miners, a restaurateur, a factory worker with the brimstone hair and hillbilly eyes of Jerry Lee Lewis. I wondered what they *meant*. What did they signify? Was it responsibility? Caring? Hard labor? Big plans? What about the wild dumbasses like my cousin Billy Joe, who won his friend's glass eye in a poker game then shot him in the ass when he tried to take it back? What about the drill sergeants, the professors, the corporate bosses?

Was the meaning of a father aggression, willfulness, knowingness, compassion? The possibilities hung like haze, and I thought maybe we should choose our fathers in dialectic pairs just to ensure balance: God and Devil; Tolstoy and Chekhov; John Lennon and Paul McCartney.

In the end I had many ersatz or partial fathers. My uncle Carl, a lawyer and former state's attorney, lived in town. He'd had my father put in jail overnight for trying to leave the area, and Carl used his political connections to try to find him when child-support checks stopped temporarily. (Department of State: "Our embassy there says no such island in the Indonesian archipelago exists.") Carl was a gentleman farmer who smelled of green peppers and insecticide, and my mom and I often returned home to find trays of sunburned strawberries or bags with ears of sweet corn weeping in their silk, with no note. His wife preferred we didn't use the kidney-shaped pool on their estate.

Doc was a cousin, old enough to have been a dentist in the Great War, who lived into the disco era. He showed love with noogies and arm burns. When he threw me a football, he hurt me, and when he took me fishing I was afraid. His patients could recall him with his knee on their chests, straining to pull teeth. Doc himself lay in a reclining chair for at least the last decade of his life, spitting amber juice from his cigar toward a bucket on the living room floor. He arrested in that chair while my mom was present. She said the paramedic pulled him out of it, put him on the floor, and began resuscitation. The corpse divulged its stomach contents into the man's mouth. I was supposed to be there too but have always been glad I wasn't.

Uncle Paul sold Fords. Sold my mom a Thunderbird she couldn't afford. He and Aunt Margie lived on the edge of the grounds of a federal veteran's hospital. The hospital was built in an odd Egyptian Revival style and stood in the middle of a parklike space amidst old oaks that Margie painted with oils. On foggy mornings I imagined that the battlefields of Europe, where Paul had fought, looked that way. My mother said they kept the "basket cases" of World War I on the top floor of the hospital, where no one could see. They were men who'd lost all their limbs, as well as sight and hearing, and a special nursing staff tended them like babies in bassinets. Paul, so vital and full of laughter that everyone called him Zip, grew barrel-chested from emphysema and eventually died in that hospital. As he slowly drowned in his own sputum, tied to bottled oxygen and a wheelchair, his eyes saddened and became perpetually wet. Aunt Margie never liked to hear "bad things."

She held her hands over her ears and sang "Dixie" if my mom tried to talk about what was going on in Vietnam. In the end my mom clipped Paul's wild thick toenails, which were yellow and ridged, while Margie made the tea.

Gary and Hank, cousins by marriage, never spoke of fatherhood at all but talked to me like equals, asked questions, played games. They were the right age in the 1960s. In the 1970s, Gary had Jim Rockford's Firebird. Hank bought one of the first water beds, a real hip cat, and once when I was showing off my new microscope he took a clean slide and went to the bathroom for a long time. Whatever was on the slide when he came back and peered at it through the eyepiece disappointed him.

As I aged and my experience accumulated, the men began to sink into other categories—big brothers, rivals, little brothers, mere acquaintances. How Not to Be: all the babies, laggards, dullards, fops, turds, and jerks of intolerance, cruelty, and self-pity.

By the time I was thirty I'd been an army diver, had married and divorced, gotten a bachelor's degree and a corporate job. I thought I knew the scope of what I didn't know. But it did strike me that among the seven billion people on this planet, many of those whom we've known—or known of—are still out there, saying and doing things: old lovers, former teachers, Vlad Putin. Mostly we interact with the *idea* of people, apparitions of memory and imagination, not the people themselves, and if we think of them at all, we act as if they live on another plane, which can't be reached from here.

But sometimes borders are opened, and one finds entry. In 1995, for instance, the U.S. began the process of rapprochement with Vietnam, and Frenchy, whom I hadn't seen in the several years since I left the service, gave me a call. He'd served in the war and was looking to triangulate his views with a return visit, and I was curious to see the place where everything began for me.

A few weeks into the trip we were in the highlands, enjoying a talk over a slow meal of gristly wild boar, sweet venison, and rice. I told him how my dad had fought in World War II, served during Korea, had been a machinist then a professor, married again after his first wife died young of cancer, became a father again at forty-five, but left us to work all over the world.

"Sounds like a hard bastard," Frenchy said. "I like him already."

I sat back, drank my beer, and thought about this new view.

~~~

My father was born in 1918, and that he would have lived long enough for the private eye I hired to find him, long-retired in south Florida, seemed unlikely. That he had, showed enormous good manners. I flew down in order to telephone, unsure what I'd do if he denied me, ignorant of what to do if he embraced me.

"You might want to sit down," I said, sitting in my pink stucco hotel across town. "I'm your son."

It was unlikely any man would have welcomed me so graciously on a Thursday evening while his third wife listened, that he wouldn't faint or curse or simply hang up. They'd been out to dinner.

"I always knew you'd call," he said. He was seventy-eight; I was thirty-three.

That he'd be smarter, better read, and more urbane than just about anyone else I knew, that he was a folk art carver, that he'd been interim president of Johnson & Wales University for a time, all seemed beyond unlikely. Think of how it might have gone. We were so much alike in our views that it did seem odd that he disliked fiction and hated photography, but he hinted at an aversion to artifice. He sat in creased slacks and a guayabera, surrounded by art and books, sipping a glass of Bordeaux. But my mom had said . . . well, a handy lesson, then: the Devil can be rich in contingent traits.

"I was just a teacher," he said as a way to cut through the knot of stories I'd been carrying all my life. Given his career, the statement seemed a soft-edged artifice, designed perhaps to ameliorate years of unpaid child support, health care, and education.

Our talk over the next years, most of it by phone, was slow, enjoyable, friendly. He and his wife had the curious, engaged, witty minds I've often wished for in acquaintances my own age. I learned my paternal grandfather had been a sharecropper, and my dad had worked in a Civilian Conservation Corps camp during the Depression. He joined the army, got out, and went to school at Illinois, went back in as an officer, and did a tour in Panama, where I'd been stationed too. Unlike me, he thought of Vietnam as just a couple of years in a busy life, but he loved Afghanistan and everything Genghis Khan. I said my army friends were sure he'd been CIA, given his timely dispatch to the troubled spots of the world and the nature of his job, which would make a good cover. He smiled.

"No. But I knew some of those guys," he said.

When my wife and I had children, we made a conscious effort to do more, committing our time and few dollars to a vacation in south Florida each stifling summer. Every morning my dad and stepmom took us to the Sunflower Café, where they'd eaten breakfast six days a week for eight years. They always bought Three Musketeers plates—sausage, egg, Mickey pancake—for our sons, who saw in the whole experience the contradictory qualities of comfort and adventure. Every night he and his wife took us to dinner. There are fortune cookie slips in my wallet even now, like uncashed checks.

The last time we flew to south Florida as a family, it was August and unbearably hot. Someone had taken down all the "Panther Crossing" signs on the airport road. Mechanical harvesters had clear-cut the sea pines and gathered them like sheaves of wheat to be taken to the paper mill. Big Cats dozed acres of sand into plots as flat and square as Midwestern farms, and cinder blocks outlined concrete pads for a new strip mall and bank. My father had been in perfect health to the age of eighty-nine. Now the doctors probed, listened, changed medicines. We worried when he walked my elder son around to show him the coconuts fallen from the palms and tracks in the mud from wild pigs.

A week or two after we left, he collapsed at the Sunflower. One of the Greek owners, George, stood over him, shouting to my ninety-year-old stepmother, "It's okay, Alix, he's breathing, he's alive!" After a few days in the hospital he went home, and we talked by phone. The doctors pronounced heart failure, and my dad said with grace and good humor we'd just have to see.

When I was called back to Florida in September, I went alone. In the Sunflower Café the waitresses sat down in booths with elderly customers to watch them shuffle photos of grandkids like decks of cards, as if looking for a good hand. Some early retirees—robust, tanned, and laughing—described the waitresses to me as "booze hags."

The women's hands shook as they poured coffee. They moved round each other in a practiced dance, hollered obscene jokes over the din, ministered with buttered toast. Three of them said they'd drop by to see my dad on their way out to the bars. They'd be off at two but were going to someone's house to shower and change first.

He was dying in a hospice room that had a view of a manmade lake with a fountain in the center. The nurses said to look for the resident gator, but the late sun made the water a mirror, and the blinds were kept shut. All I could do was run little errands, be calm, and talk about his grandsons. I couldn't share much more in his life, but I wanted to show I cared enough . . . to be hard enough . . . to witness his dying.

There weren't many left to bear witness. Most of his friends and colleagues from various universities and from his years abroad had been dead for years. A few more lived far away. I was a little afraid for him, with his failed breath, and for his wife, who couldn't hear, and it had something to do with loneliness. Sentimental, perhaps, since the dying often distance themselves long before they die, but I was still thankful when neighbors came, chatted, and left.

My father was glad to see the waitresses when they came in loudly, smelling of perfume, smokes, and the gin they'd had before they left the house. Their faces looked harder and more worn, the disappointments more obvious, now they were made up to go out. They cooed and smiled, and one was missing teeth. They were very beautiful.

They sat around the bed and caught him up on all the news from the Sunflower. George was *still* an asshole and took advantage. One of them had walked out after another shouting match with him then walked back in the next day. A former waitress, whom my dad and his wife might have remembered, had finally lost everything—hard drugs, they said—and had gone away with nowhere to go.

They'd been there half an hour before they realized my father didn't have the breath to speak. He was embarrassed and frustrated, so I told them about his work for USAID in Vietnam and Afghanistan, his job as an advisor in the tin mines in Indonesia, the sabbatical he'd done in Paris at a lost-wax gold foundry.

"Oh, isn't that interesting," they said. "You do get around, don't you, Hon?"

They could see he was tiring, so they said their last goodbyes. They were headed out to the beach, where there were drink specials. I had to go in the bathroom while they kissed him and patted his hands and said see you at the restaurant soon.

My entire childhood, my mom told me that when I grew up to be big and strong I'd find my dad and beat him up for her. At the end of her life she bragged that he was a big strapping man whose team members did what he said, no b.s., boy.

He was two inches taller than me, and even at eighty-nine, and after two months of wasting, he was heavy. He kept sliding down in the motorized bed that propped him up, and the bedclothes twisted and bunched at his feet. When I couldn't manage to move him back, I tried to help him sit up. The skin on his back was papery, loose over hard muscle and bone. I was afraid I'd hurt him, but it took some force just to jam pillows behind him. Other than a handshake, it was the first time I'd touched his flesh. The next morning there were large purple hemorrhages where my palms had been and where he'd leaned against the bedrail. They put him on a drug cocktail to keep the panic from rising as water filled his lungs. Offshore, the shallows blackened with algae blooms.

Since my father didn't like artifice, I didn't say see you soon, feel better. I kissed his face, a first and last time for everything, and said other things. He wanted to tell me something but didn't have the breath. I said his wife could tell me later. He smiled and respected me enough not to nod.

I had breakfast at the Sunflower one last time, the morning I flew home. The three graces were supposed to be working, but only two had made it in, and I said it was nice to see them again and thanked them for everything. When I went to pay at the counter, George, who mans the register eternally, asked how much I wanted to tip. The bill was ten bucks, and I said to add five.

George dismissed me. "That is too much. Two dollars, that's enough," he said in his accent and started to punch in numbers on the credit card machine.

"No," I said firmly. "You've all been very kind." He was bald with a fringe, in his fifties, and had soft-boiled eyes.

We stood awkwardly while the transaction went through.

"We are sorry about everything that has happened," he said finally. He ripped the receipt off and put it down for me to sign. "But what can you say? There is nothing to be done. We are born to die."

〜〜〜

Two days later my family and I were on a train to Chicago for a day at the museum. My phone rang. I answered, looked at Mrs. Churm, sitting across the aisle with Wolfie in her lap, and shook my head. She turned to the window and began to cry. Starbuck, whose real name is John, same as my father and me, lay asleep with his head on my legs, and I stroked his hair.

Who will protect us from the news? As a child, I feared loss, unaware it was already present in the absence of my father, in a family too old to remain for long, in the vacancies of poverty and its empty glosses. A world of ghosts, past and present.

But death is only part of the story, friends, and it's time to exorcise partial stories. Let's set down fear like a heavy bag and shoulder instead a more complex understanding.

Late that night, my wife asked what I was feeling, and I said it was complicated. I loved my father for ten years, after hating and fearing the idea of him for more than three decades. I was grieving, but I wondered aloud if he was standing in the lunch line in Hell.

〜〜〜

I never knew my father as a father, but as something else, for a short, late time. As a result, my two sons have exactly as much experience with actual fatherhood as I do. What we've learned together is that fathers are mercurial, full of farts and orders, radiant with heat on a summer's night already too hot for sleep. Fathers love words and pay children the compliment of deep attentiveness. They're who you call for when you wake in pain. They cultivate the comforting myth of invincibility. Even in the manner of their deaths we learn something specific.

In our own knowledge and memories, not others', there's a finishing effect, a maturing, acceptance, that makes it possible to continue and become. This is not inevitable. Many never approach what they must be. To be, among other things—as unlikely as it might have seemed to me growing up—a father.

The College of Hard Knocks

Remember the scene in Disney's *Pinocchio* where the wooden boy jumps into the sea to look for his father, who's been swallowed by a giant whale named Monstro? It strikes me how well the animators understood and portrayed the way that bodies move underwater. Maybe master animator Milt Kahl's reputed obsession with getting the art right led him to observe deep-sea divers; at the least I'm convinced he was once a great swimmer.

Knowledge of the physical world is one of the things I value in writing, however it manifests, because it almost always leads to psychological and emotional truths. The image in the poem "In Your Honor," by Arthur Sze, of "a sea bass / tied to a black-lacquered dish by green-spun seaweed," its eye "clear and luminous," the way it "smells / of dream, but this is no dream," and how it "bleeds and flaps, bleeds and flaps as / the host slices slice after slice of glistening sashimi," is immediate, memorable, and visceral—cutting, no less—in a way that the literary equivalent of conceptual art, or sound for sound's sake, rarely is for me. Our best and most enduring writers find their own solutions, even in the most interior writing, to the mind-body problem.

Of course if we end up digitizing the world one day, natural things and processes may become moot. For now a piece in the *Times* worries, "What will so many alternative realities do to the one in which we live?"

One thing they seemed to do at Hinterland was affect student writing. Characters often moved through pixelated-prose landscapes with odd movements—not the motion of dreams, which has its own natural law, but in jerky and inconsequential ways—as if mimicking bad video-game graphics or fanboy ways of love.

"Some must work in fields," said Thoreau, "if only for the sake of tropes and expression, to serve a parable-maker one day." Call it reactionary (Rory will, though he'll recant privately) to regret the loss of old tropes, but I often saw young writers whose work suffered because they had no metaphors with which to think.

Many hadn't had much direct contact with the natural world. They'd never seen a snake eat another snake or a grackle pull strips of red muscle from the wren under its foot. They'd never raised a crop through a tedious season or been forced to keep swimming because to stop would mean death.

Protected by technologies, many had never known inescapable cold or heat; supported by affluence, they'd never known real hunger or thirst. They worked fast food or retail, occupations short on specialized processes and tools; they rode in cars sealed against breeze (who can take a seventy-five-mile-per-hour breeze?) and road noise; they ran on treadmills in the corner of a gym, iPod earbuds turned up loud so they couldn't hear their own panting, or the thump of blood.

I remember an undergrad workshop with three students like this. The first had written a story about kids fooling around near a "mansion." There were few details—a problem in itself—but what was there was false. I felt it, because the neighborhood didn't sound right for a mansion, whatever that might mean. During Socratic questioning, it was revealed the writer meant, simply, a Victorian house, though he'd never heard the term. How big was it? I asked. How old? Was it frame or brick? Did it have gingerbread? None of that mattered directly to the story, but he couldn't begin to imagine his way into it because he didn't know the consequences of his chosen setting.

I explained how my neighborhood was a mix of various styles, built over 150 years. I did a bit on post-and-beam versus balloon frames in our area, and how the former required craftsmanship that the latter didn't, which meant expense back then to build it and, paradoxically, less demand for it now, so the struggling middle class bought the old places and . . . ah, yes, we do need to continue class. I suggested he at least walk around town to try to find the words he'd need to describe the neighborhood he had in mind. Fictional characters, like the living, have a hard time living in abstractions.

The second student desperately needed details for two characters cooking a meal together. "I don't know how people make food," he said, looking
surprised and rueful at his own admission.

"Come to my house and I'll show you how to cook a meal," I said. The
class laughed because they thought I was playing the fool. I often play the
fool, but I meant it. Cooking has taught me more ways to think about writing than all the how-to books combined.

The third student had (what I consider) a problem in his writing common to many young men in my classes—a fetish for cartoonish, melodra-
matic violence. It boasted a pornography of rich details about shattering the
kneecaps of a guy stretched across a table yet didn't consider human pain as
a topic, let alone take up the emotions involved in revenge. As I do sometimes when I get frustrated with this tendency, I recounted how young men
in love with the idea of violence stood in lines around the block to enlist
for the Great War. In London, Paris, Berlin, no one wanted to miss the
grand adventure. It would be a lark, and they'd be home in a few months
with tales to tell their children someday. Several million dead later—nearly
a generation of potential leaders, scientists, artists, teachers, parents wiped
out—those young men didn't regard it so merrily. And I didn't say this,
but I cannot imagine anyone who's known pain—anyone human, that is—
writing lovingly about torture. Our bodies are our first metaphors.

〜〜〜

Everybody in the academy wants to talk about the Other. Wants to talk
about Hegel. Wants to talk about Sartre. I want to talk about the carrot.

I don't mean those slick little buggers the size of my pinky fingers, bred
for the lathe that planes them smooth and skinless. They're oversweet and
tender, and I eat them by the pound while I'm writing. But I made the
mistake recently of putting them in a stew, where they blanched and grew
spongy.

I mean real carrots, which teach you about hierarchies of forces, most of
them beyond your control. A real carrot—I'm eating one now—is shocking.
It is what it is: a texture all its own, flavor that's not-quite-earth and not-
quite-woods, with the strong aroma of anise. Like a real tomato, so hard to
find in stores now, it's food for those who want to taste life.

This is probably why our society has been sold on the idea of paying a 5,000 percent markup on bottles of water. Most of them taste like *something*, whether it's the aftertaste of vomit or the nostalgia of cold cast iron.

This is what we know, so it's how we think.

In a paper in the proceedings of the 2007 Ohio Valley Philosophy of Education Society, scholar Bryan R. Warnick sums up the emphasis Ralph Waldo Emerson places on an education in the natural world:

> First, Emerson argues that nature offers the possibility of solitude and, with this solitude, comes silence. The silence allows for the emergence of "voices" that are otherwise marginalized in the dominant technological society. Second, in nature there are unique possibilities for the development of moral thought through distinctive nontechnological metaphors. Third, nature forces us both to see difference and to develop our sense of "worship," that is, it promotes a feeling that there is an Other, a "not-me," who is worthy of respect. Fourth, a proper educative relationship with nature allows us to escape the ethical dissonance that can come from being complicit in the destructive forces of modern economies, and, at the same time, to develop our talents as human beings. These four modes of natural education are not separate, however, but converge on the idea of "justice." The education of nature is about coming to understand our place in and our connections to the world. To understand this is to understand what justice requires.

This specialized meaning of justice might be an alternative or addendum to what William Gass calls writer John Gardner's "cranky" ideas about "moral" fiction, which Gardner defined partly as inevitable surprises of consequence.

Seamus Heaney's final poetry collection, *Human Chain*, contains these lines:

> And now . . . Jonah entering
> The whale's mouth, as the Old English says,
> Like a mote through a minster door.

How beautiful and perfect this image of swallowment by the abyss, the vulgar dust of man drifting into the immensity of the divine, a sublime descent to a place where one's Father awaits (as with both Pinocchio and Aeneas): all metaphor, and all tied to the things of the world and their relations.

Are the metaphors of humility, distance, scale, love becoming less accessible to us all the time? I have motes in my old couch, waiting to be beaten out, and motes in my eye, ditto, but who ever mentions them? What with the state of the economy, prefab technologies, and standardized building codes, most doors we travel through are the same door, from motel to morgue.

I was discussing all this with Frenchy, who embodies to me the Emerson quote, "Common sense is genius dressed in its working clothes." He selflessly devised a solution for my creative-writing students—he was willing to found a college up on his mountain, devoted to this idea by Thoreau:

> Speaking about education: I mean that [students] should not play life, or study it merely, while the community supports them at this expensive game, but earnestly live it from beginning to end. How could youths better learn to live than by at once trying the experiment of living? Methinks this would exercise their minds as much as mathematics. If I wished a boy to know something about the arts and sciences, for instance, I would not pursue the common course, which is merely to send him into the neighborhood of some professor, where anything is professed and practiced but the art of life;—to survey the world through a telescope or a microscope, and never with his natural eye; to study chemistry, and not learn how his bread is made, or mechanics, and not learn how it is earned; to discover new satellites to Neptune, and not detect the motes in his eyes, or to what vagabond he is a satellite himself; or to be devoured by the monsters that swarm all around him, while contemplating the monsters in a drop of vinegar.

At Snowshoe College of West Virginia, Frenchy would teach aspiring writers discipline, sacrifice, and content, mostly by having them fell dead trees on his property, cut them into eighteen-inch lengths, and split them into cordwood with a maul. He could manage six or seven handpicked students at a time, three men and four women, he specified for some reason.

"I need at least seven ricks of wood to make it through the winter," he said. "Eight would be better in case it's a cold spring. Tell 'em to dress warm and bring their own food. I've got one extra bed; the rest sleep on the floor."

Upon graduation, he asserted, students would have gained the knowledge of the names of tools and the processes of their maintenance and use;

an understanding of mass and weight; the consequences of the ache of muscle and sharp pinch of blisters; they'd know what it meant to inhabit a body pushed past endurance; they'd have memories of the taste of food seasoned by hunger, and the sights and sounds of the mountain and river and trees. They'd have the smell of wood smoke to write about.

"If nothing else, they'll understand despotism," he said.

It's unusual for someone who graduated from a college to go on to teach there, but I was Frenchy's employee once and have continued to work with him over the years, so who's better qualified? But there'll be a prerequisite for my courses: students will need to have raised chickens and sold the eggs to pay for my lattes up at the ski resort, where I'll be waiting to critique drafts of their writing, should they have the time or energy left over to write them. This too is an allegory.

Languor

It's a feeling I've known since childhood, though it's come only sporadically over the years: an extreme sleepiness without fatigue, a dream without sleep, a staggering drunk without the buzz, a codeine high without skin rash. My eyes won't focus; I stumble. Usually it occurs in summertime or in the tropics or subtropics, but not every hot climate causes it, and sometimes I sink into it in some cool interior such as a public library.

Melville describes the feeling, which he attributes to languor, washing over everyone aboard the ship *Dolly*:

> We abandoned the fore-peak altogether, and spreading an awning over the forecastle, slept, ate, and lounged under it the live-long day. Every one seemed to be under the influence of some narcotic. Even the officers aft, whose duty required them never to be seated while keeping a deck watch, vainly endeavoured to keep on their pins; and were obliged invariably to compromise the matter by leaning up against the bulwarks, and gazing abstractedly over the side. Reading was out of the question; take a book in your hand, and you were asleep in an instant.

In the army we called it Brain Fever. For two or three days at a time we'd lie around like lotus eaters, missing meals, going unwashed, shirking our duties as dutifully as we could. The worst case I ever had was after jumping off a Blackhawk somewhere near Río Coclé del Norte, in the Republic of Panama, expecting to join my dive detachment but finding I'd beat them there. I spent a soporific week by myself in an otherwise empty 16' × 32' tent belonging to a larger unit bivouacked high above the sea. It was hot and windy at night and hotter and more humid in the day, and I spent both days and nights sleeping or nearly asleep in that canvas tent, plagued by mosquitoes and weird dreams, and pacing like a sleepwalker.

In the middle of one of those surreal nights a young PFC from the engineer battalion apparently walked off the cliff, fell several stories onto volcanic boulders, and was swept away by the breakers. When I was shaken awake roughly by fellow soldiers shining their flashlights in my eyes, they called me by his name, hoping upon hope he wasn't sunk in that black sea. There were many rumors as to what really happened to him, but I've wondered all these years if it was death by languor.

It has occurred to me that languor is a type of depression, though it feels nothing like the loss of the magic of adventure, when foreign mountains are suddenly just mountains, and not like being in love. I used to get it when I visited my sister's home, where I felt unusually safe, and it interfered with my visit.

I've also wondered if it might be useful, a protective mechanism to slow me down the way a bad summer cold will do when I've been working too hard, a way for the subconscious to get more time to work. Even when I fall asleep on the couch after dinner and pick my way through conversations like a dullard, I sometimes try to indulge the languor, if I have time or the ability, because it feels necessary. I also look for the thing that signals the end of it.

A few months ago, in the midst of a languor misty enough to make my freshly painted walls drip, I got an unexpected e-mail from an old army friend, who led me to another. I hadn't seen or spoken to Egg or Sammy since the early 1980s, and it seems odd to say they've been my lifelong friends, since I only knew them one or two years, a quarter of a century ago. But my memories of them are so plentiful and strong—confirmed now by speaking with them—that the people they were then have been with me since young adulthood, and something awful that Sammy did even showed up on page ninety-five of my first novel.

And so—just as I was getting back to work on a novel set in the Gulf of Mexico, recently deep in oil, about a group of veterans looking for one of their own and pulling into a Florida city with blighted real estate—here, up from out of the languor, swam my old friends, one of whom was an engineer on a Coast Guard tug during the *Exxon Valdez* disaster and knew all about spills and salvage, and the other who lived in that blighted city and had a girlfriend in the chief mortgage/title business there. Those were wonderful, odd coincidences—nay, a sign from the universe to snap out of it and work harder—but that's not all.

We leave our suitcases in other people's houses. They keep them for us, sometimes, even after we've left word to throw them out. Much later, to our dreamlike amazement, the cases are brought to us, opened, and we get to measure ourselves against what we remember being. Some part of us has been saved when we thought it was lost, and we realize we're carried around as we carry others within. It's reason enough to rouse ourselves and get moving.

We Transit

Rolled by breakers, weightless but confused, Gulliver washes ashore. Stands up in the surf, heavy and off-balance, backwash pulling strongly at his shins, can't get a footing in the fluid sands of a new country.

⌇⌇⌇

Sometimes our ambitions are big enough that they pull others into our orbits. My then-girlfriend moved to Miami with me so I could do grad work, and her folks, Margaret and Fred, retired to Fort Myers to be near their daughter, their only child.

⌇⌇⌇

The HMS *Bounty*, in transit from Connecticut to Florida, sinks in Hurricane Sandy, ninety miles southeast of Cape Hatteras. Two Coast Guard MH-60 Jayhawks arrive in the dark, turbines screaming, lights aglow, convex-eyed insects in the maelstrom. Dark water rolls in from every direction, thirty-foot swells, a rescue swimmer in the lead chopper says it's like looking into the agitator of a washing machine. They orbit two life rafts in the water; one man in a Gumby suit floats separately at a distance. The hoist operator names him, in the calm speech of the well trained, "the free-floating gentleman."

Wouldn't it be a comfort if we knew our gods spoke with the same professionalism and respect?

~~~

When I met my mother- and father-in-law to be in 1994, they'd already lived two entire lives. They were from Inverness, Scotland, originally. Fred was a little too young in World War II to fight on the continent, so he served in the Home Guard instead. The rest of his regiment was trapped at Dunkirk and taken prisoner by the Germans. Margaret was in the postwar Royal Navy. She and Fred had lived in England, the Highlands, and the Orkneys before immigrating to Chicago in the late 1950s. Margaret worked as a dental assistant and then for many years as an accounts manager for a food-service conglomerate. Fred was a dental technician and made appliances and prosthetics, and after a while he had a basement workshop in their home, so he was able to provide childcare for their daughter. When we met he had advanced emphysema from breathing the plaster dust of his trade. They had lovely stories to tell about the Scots community in Chicago, and how one time Fred brought home a touring Canadian pipe band that had been playing at the local mall. It took multiple trips in his car to get them all to their house, but there was music and laughter and good scotch whiskey till the wee hours.

~~~

Louisiana isn't the same South as lower Alabama, for example. Softer, and sometimes I hear Tidewater-like accents. The kindness of a courtly, sympathetic, older man, his wish that children be in peace and grow to be strong, is enough to cause tears.

~~~

Fred died in Fort Myers, a place I don't think he ever really liked and certainly had never planned to live. Accompanying his wife and daughter, I carried his ashes through airports and placed them in a hole in an ancient cemetery on a hill overlooking Beauly Firth. At his wake I met his old friend Tommy McDonald, one of the men taken prisoner by the Germans at Dunkirk. He was a comical, randy old man with terrific hair, chatting up all the widows and telling stories he acted out with a glass in his hand. He's dead now too.

~~~

The young barber looks very southern. How do I mean that? It's in his eyes and styled into his own hair, inspiration of pompadour. The low, old-fashioned establishment is just off campus, a barber's pole outside, the barbers often unoccupied. He greets me so enthusiastically that he forgets to ask me to sit and begins to prepare his tools while I stand awkwardly in the entry. His electric trimmers are dull and yank my short hair, but I'm afraid to move. He makes hard work of it, so he has plenty of time to tell me he's not a reader, but he picked up a book the other day and couldn't put it down, it was just really great, and I should read it. He wants to know if I've heard of historical fiction, and I say I've heard of it. Have I heard of the author? I haven't and ask what period it's set in, though I have an idea. Civil War, he says enthusiastically, or just after. A soldier gets home and finds his house has been messed with, his mother and sister raped. Dad's dying wish is that the young man get revenge, so he does. Along the way there are adventures, excitement, love—the book has it *all*.

~~~

It wasn't always perfect, but what is? She and Fred hadn't been given the chance to go to college, and I often puzzled them. She said more than once that I didn't have a real job because I wasn't in an office every day, 8:30–5:00. When I opened the box with copies of my newly published second book, I handed her the first one and said thank you for all she'd done to help around the house while I wrote it.

"Every time you look at that you'll think: another wasted summer," Margaret said. "Mother!" my wife cried.

Critics.

~~~

Apparently there was a large contingent of Jayhawkers in this area:

The Civil War became known as "a rich man's war and a poor man's fight." While the Confederate government championed the cause of States' Rights, many poor Southerners soon viewed it as a war to preserve the institution of slavery, and hence the way of life of the wealthy planter class that slavery permitted to flourish. . . . While a few of South Louisiana's French Acadians belonged to the planter class, most of them were poor farmers, who depended for farm labor on their own large families, and who regarded the conflict as "the American war" (*la guerre de les Américains*). . . . The ranks of the Louisiana Jayhawkers reached their peak around March 1864, and included recruits of every persuasion—deserters from Texas and Louisiana, draft dodgers, free Negroes and escaped slaves, some of whom continued to fight even after General Lee surrendered. (W. T. Block, "Some Notes on the Civil War Jayhawkers of Confederate Louisiana")

Somehow this makes me feel more at home.

~~~

By our request, Margaret followed us again, to central Illinois, and moved into an apartment across town, where she often cared for our two sons in turn so they didn't have to go full-time to daycare. No matter where she was, she couldn't just sit, and her visits were never, not once, just visits. We'd beg her not to do our laundry or clean our house, but even after she'd had an embolism and her lung function was diminished, she'd practically jog, breathless, to get it all done.

"Mother," my wife would warn.

Margaret had long-practiced ways to do exactly what she wanted to do.

"Don't fuss," she'd say with her remaining trace of Invernesian accent. "I just have this one last little thing, and then that's it, I promise."

~~~

A fraternity, whose "spiritual founder" is Robert E. Lee. The boys wear their mixer T-shirts, on the back of which is a poorly executed drawing of a Confederate officer with his hoop-skirted woman, standing chastely, fingers-to-fingers, in front of a manor house. The caption is about a man's honor above all.

~~~

An enormous moon over loblolly pines. Antediluvian fogs in the dark dripping mornings. The weird trills of boat-tailed grackles, who drag their over-
long tail feathers around parking lots, asking about something.

~~~

My wife and sons and I drove down to Louisiana to look for a house.
Margaret was to come along but didn't feel well enough to travel. Soon
after we returned she was diagnosed with stage IV pancreatic cancer. When
we moved to Louisiana for good, there was no question she'd move with us
and live in our new house. Despite the upheaval, discomfort, and pain that
the move would mean for her, we wanted as much time as possible with her,
especially for the sake of my sons, who loved her beyond measure.

~~~

Three months after my mother died, in Illinois, she appeared alive, in a
photograph taken in Louisiana, on the front page of *USA Today*. I was leaving the lobby of a hotel and froze when I saw the photo through the acrylic
window in the newspaper box. Hurricane Katrina had just occurred, and
the gaunt old woman, her face distorted with grief, was being pulled across
the flood in a johnboat.

I don't mean that the woman in the photo looked like my mother. I mean
it was my mother. She was crying because death had made her lonesome.

I've never said anything before about that photo of my mother crossing
the Styx. It's unusual for the press to cover the event, and of course I haven't
been able to find the photo again, anywhere, not even in the online museum
of newspaper front pages. I *think* it was *USA Today*.

~~~

I'm sure as hell not from central Illinois, where I lived and taught for more
than a decade. I'm not from Chicago, either, though I married there, twice,
and lived in its suburbs and across northern Illinois for twenty years. I'm not
from Florida, Virginia, Kentucky, California, or the Republic of Panama,
though I've lived each of those places for months or years.

I'm not from other places I've visited—Europe, the UK, Guatemala.

I'm not from Vietnam, where I was born, though my bones, brain, and blood were formed with its water and minerals. I am from southern Illinois, which I always thought was more of the South than of the North, though when I try to go home again I'm no longer of it, exactly.

Like many these days, I've been in long motion and often enjoyed it. I am uprooted, which is to say only that I'm a modern, and an American without hereditary wealth.

~~~

The girls in their prom dresses colored like angelfish, scarlet ibises, blue morphos, gather on the courthouse lawn to have their photos taken at the base of the statue of the Confederate soldier. Its plinth is inscribed, "The South's Defenders / 1861–1865 / Our Heroes."

~~~

We got a landline again, the first in years, so Margaret could talk to old friends in Britain. There weren't many of her generation left. She lost all interest in TV and read book after book. She made herself oatmeal every morning but mostly lived on nutrition shakes. The pain grew and then grew unmanageable. On Tuesday that week she and I were in the house alone, and she called out for me.

She'd been in the hospital two days when we talked with her and the shift supervisor from hospice about getting a hospital bed in our home, a bedside commode if necessary, a walker for the long hallway, and a wheelchair when it became needed. Her hearing had gone, and the man had a soft Louisiana voice, so she didn't understand most of it. She apologized to us and said she didn't want to be a bother. I translated for the man, who'd said it was their belief the whole family was the patient. I said all I needed for myself was to know that she didn't feel a bother, that she was our family, that this was her home. She told my wife that she would try to do this for my sake, since I'd asked, and my wife, who'd insisted on this for years, had to laugh. The boys gave her stuffed animals to sleep with and said goodnight and we love you.

~~~

Wendell Berry in his recent Jefferson lecture, on affection for place as a moral force:

> Always in human history there have been costly or catastrophic sudden changes. But with relentless fanfare, at the cost of almost indescribable ecological and social disorder, and to the almost incalculable enrichment and empowerment of corporations, industrialists have substituted what they fairly accurately call "revolution" for the slower, kinder processes of adaptation or evolution. . . . It is true that these revolutions have brought some increase of convenience and comfort and some easing of pain. It is also true that the industrialization of everything has incurred liabilities and is running deficits that have not been adequately accounted . . . [including] a social condition which apologists call "mobility," implying that it has been always "upward" to a "higher standard of living," but which in fact has been an ever-worsening unsettlement of our people, and the extinction or near-extinction of traditional and necessary communal structures.

~~~

Two cell phones and the landline popped off in the dark middle of that same night, lights flashing, different ringtones a cacophony of confusion. My wife raced for the hospital, but her mother was gone before she got there. I woke the boys at four a.m. to take them to the hospital, saying only that Grandma needed us. They were sleepy, it was dark, the ride silent, but they didn't fall back to sleep. My wife met us in the hallway. In the room I held Wolfie in my arms, big enough now his feet hung down to my knees, and he couldn't lay his head on my shoulder anymore. He and Starbuck didn't want to leave the body. We had thought we had until Thanksgiving, maybe even Christmas. In the corridor I caught Starbuck staring at posters of green-clad, Klan-looking, Mardi Gras mummers, very spooky; I hoped the image wouldn't remain in his memory of that night.

In Vietnam once, a van I was riding in passed through a defunct rubber plantation. I saw a cemetery there with a solitary French Catholic grave among scores of Vietnamese Buddhist tombs and had the lonely vision of a French ghost watching Vietnamese ghosts play cards at a distance and talk together by the sea, forever.

It still worries at me.

The funeral home in this new and slightly strange place was very large and almost beautiful, a brick building with twenty-foot ceilings, hand-adzed plank floors, and full-length mirrors that could have come from a manor house or a French chateau. It had a full kitchen for in-house catering. But our rituals were not theirs. Because there are so many Catholics, the director explained, there had been very few cremations. Because so many had their own clergy, it was unusual that we asked him to arrange for someone, and of course Presbyterian means something entirely different here than in Scotland.

The minister was "independent," he said. He was white-haired, leathery, and very respectful not only of the death but also our position as outsiders in this world of crayfish, rice, and oil. She lay on an improvised bier made from a rolling stainless-steel morgue table. The boys cried, Goodbye, Grandma, which ripped me to shreds. Starbuck did that for my mother, and I hear in it, Goodbye childhood, goodbye innocence, goodbye my understanding that love can endure in a single body through time.

We came back to the house and there was an Ensure bottle placed strangely in the middle of the living room floor. Though I felt a jolt of the uncanny, I quickly blamed the dog, for Wolfie's sake, because he started to get upset in the same way that Starbuck had demanded loudly to know why we thought the doctor should have called after Margaret's death.

"What would he have to say?" Starbuck had asked, desperate with hope for reversal.

Enduring memories that float in just when we're hopelessly overwhelmed, images presenting themselves without our trying to perceive or place into words:

Outside the hospital, the hour or so after Margaret dies, some beat-up orange tabby with no tail, the tail gone, just a ridiculous root-end of a tail, and a mutilated ear. His tough tomcat demeanor, a mythopoetic type familiar the world over, a carnal distillation of the life force itself, all furry balls and catcalls, this small tiger, this rapscallion, this pirate, gliding past silly humans dragging toward their cars in a parking lot. Starbuck and I watch him slinking along, self-important, places to go; he shoots us a disdainful glare over his shoulder. Starbuck and I look at each other, and without forethought or guilt, and for some reason I cannot imagine, my son and I laugh aloud at the same time. That free feline gentleman hears us and disappears in the box-leafed holly.

Repose

Dick said no American men had any repose, except himself, and they were
seeking an example to confront him with. . . .

    In another unseated party a man endlessly patted his shaven cheek with
his palm, and his companion mechanically raised and lowered the stub
of a cold cigar. The luckier ones fingered eyeglasses and facial hair, the
unequipped stroked blank mouths, or even pulled desperately at the lobes
of their ears. . . .

    "You see," said Dick smugly, "I'm the only one."

    —F. SCOTT FITZGERALD, *Tender Is the Night*

All that desperate fingering / stroking / pulling at hair / cheeks / mouths /
lobes—observed by someone named Dick Diver—only sounds like a reference to the monthly orgy on the yacht of one of my publishers, to which
I'm never invited. Really the passage is about appearing to be self-possessed
even when you're cracking up—doubly important if the other chaps at
Princeton judged you because you hail from St. Paul, Minnesota.

    Fitzgerald's repose, a class notion that rejects the body as vulgar, is not
insignificant. Think of Nixon's sweaty jowls in his debates with Kennedy,
or the panther scream of politician Howard Dean. But true repose, if it's
achievable, is not posturing. Thoreau describes it in *Walden*:

    Let us settle ourselves, and work and wedge our feet downward through the
    mud and slush of opinion, and prejudice, and tradition, and delusion, and
    appearance, that alluvion which covers the globe . . . till we come to a hard

bottom . . . which we call reality, and say, This is, and no mistake . . . below freshet and frost and fire, a place where you might found a wall or state, or set a lamp-post safely.

He got the idea from Emerson, who points back to Plato: "The problem of philosophy is . . . to find a ground unconditioned and absolute." It's the place that makes possible any number of things—independence, selfhood, seeing clearly. But how to get there?

〰

It was finals week at Hinterland, and students were permitting their parents to drive three hours south to pick them up for a summer at home. Outside one residence hall a dad in expensive shorts barked orders at his son's friends humping stereo components to the car. Mother, in her nylon tracksuit, did the cha-cha of uselessness, trying to be helpful but also getting yelled at by her husband as if she were a child. Several younger parents in the drive seemed eager to relive their own college glory; they shouted to each other and giggled and went into football stances and paced up the block, evidently looking for the Skulls kegger. An older mom and dad trudged from dorm to curb, hardly looking up; their demeanor said, It's OK, run over my feet again with your wheeled Vuitton luggage, I'm of no great consequence anyhow. All the students were embarrassed and begged to get on the road. It's an awkward time.

Disengaging suddenly and finally from my students each semester fills me with nervous energy. I walked to, and from, and then back to, campus—more than four miles—for no good reason other than to focus my eyes on something more distant than a page of student writing.

〰

Do you have repose? Take the Patillo test. It's named for an army friend who used to try to annoy us by always asking, "Ain't you itchin'?"

"No," we replied, even when covered in ticks and leeches and dying the death of a thousand cuts from saw grass.

"Bet you are," Patillo said. "Bet you're itchin' right now. Huh? You itchin'? Up there on your scalp? Top of your left ear?"

"Hell we are," we replied.

"Oh, yes you are, you can't help it," Patillo said. "It's just a little tickle, but it's growing, isn't it? Now it's on your right shoulder blade, and it itches like hell. Jesus, it's on your lip. Scratch it. Scratch at it. You know you want to. You got to. It's in the hair on your shin, it's like you got fleas and they're bitin' you. They brought the mosquitoes with 'em. And the earwax is in on it; it's tickling the little hairs in your ear canal; my God, it's the most sensitive place on your body. Scratch it! Rub it! Git it!"

Last I heard of Patillo, he was training helicopter pilots. Imagine yourself wrestling the collective, the cyclic, and both pedals on a big turbocharged aircraft known in aviation circles—due to its capriciousness—as the DeathJet Ranger. It's been painted bright orange so it'll be easier to find from the air when it crashes. Sweat runs into your eyes, where you can't reach it under your helmet visor, even if you could take your hands from the controls. Your instructor, Warrant Officer Patillo, tells you you're doing fine.

Then: "Hey, are you itchin'?"

If you can say confidently that you wouldn't be affected, you may have repose.

〰

At some point every semester, a student asks, "Why is literature always about bad stuff?" It's a good question, since that perception keeps so many—especially those in the middle class who want only happyhappy—from art. Part of the answer is that drama is conflict.

So we've heated up the earth, and the last of the polar bears may be gone within twenty-five years. So what? In the cosmic view, it's no big deal, but I have a hard time with it. And you know who's next, after the polar bears: your third-grade teacher, Miss Benzene, that great hulk in polymer pearls who for years dressed her snarling Chihuahua in little red pants, a fur-lined jacket, and a Santa hat, and brought him to school the last day before winter break. She slapped Danny Tule, the littlest kid in class, right out of his desk for bragging about being a tap dancer while she was trying to explain the pageantry of the birth of the Christ child.

Miss Benzene, god love her, finally retired to Boca last year. She's ninety-eight. Too mean to die and too stubborn to move back to the Midwest, she too will be washed out of being in another fifty years or so.

"Get the hell out of my Florida room!" she'll yell at the Atlantic as it rises against her, but the waves, as salty as tears, will lap over her and the fourteenth incarnation of her hateful rat dog anyway.

I'll have to find and text Danny Tule from the nursing home I'll be in by then, to tell him there's justice after all. The cosmic narrator, who has ultimate repose, will yawn and chug a quart of neutrinos right from the carton.

⌇

I've always felt repose was possible, else what's a minor in philosophy for? But loss is an obstacle. When events throw you off balance or give you pause, how can you be "below freshet and frost"? I'll never get over the fact that I won't play pool with Sam Clemens, or that I didn't catch Mozart live in London on his European tour of 1764. I wholeheartedly regret that my writing didn't make me rich and somewhat famous until now, so I never got to do coke off a toilet seat with Mick and Bianca at Studio 54, or use my influence to be an extra in the film *Magical Mystery Tour*.

I grew up thinking of the Beatles as the older brothers I never had, though John and Paul were already fathers when I was born. Now my sons love them too. Starbuck knew all the words to "Yellow Submarine" when he turned three, and his favorite curse was "Aw, Bonka!" (It referred to the Apple Bonkers, the Blue Meanies' skinny henchmen.)

One day not so long after my mother's funeral, Starbuck asked, "Daddy? Are the Beatles alive?"

I instantly saw his new understanding of things. "The Beatles don't play as a group anymore," I said, dodging.

"But where do they live?"

"Oh, Paul lives in England, I guess. Ringo is more of an LA guy. Vegas, maybe."

Then he had me. "What about John? And George? Where do they live?"

I hesitated. He was our first child, after all; how does one answer, except honestly?

"They died," I said.

"John and George died?" he asked.

"Yes," I said.

That was all he seemed to need to know for several weeks, but I knew there were harder questions ahead. Grandma Helen had died, we told him, because she was very old and very sick. It was true enough, and he needed reassurance that my wife and I wouldn't die for a long time and neither would he. So that became the rule for him: you got very old, and very sick, and *then*, maybe, you could die. But to Starbuck, John Lennon was the handsome young man in *A Hard Day's Night* who bats his eyes at the British banker and says, "Give us a kiss." It wouldn't help any to tell him that Lennon was younger than I was when he died.

It came on the way home from his school. We were laughing at John's high-pitched shouting ("Yassuh! Take one, the United Jumbo Band!") at the start of a bootleg version of "Ob-La-Di, Ob-La-Da." I replayed it several times so we could mimic it well.

Unexpectedly, Starbuck asked, "Did John die?"

"Yes," I said and let the music play.

"Did he get old and die? Was he sick?"

I tried to make my voice matter-of-fact—a sort of cruelty, I felt, which meant that I was so callous that I could abide the horrific, and that he would be asked to do so too—and said, "No, a man hurt him."

"How?"

"The man shot him with a gun. He hurt John so badly that he couldn't stay alive."

"Oh," Starbuck said.

Of course, I didn't tell him the accounts I'd read of John alone in the backseat of the New York City Police car that sped him from the Dakota in an attempt to save his life. A policeman named Moran turned and asked, "Are you John Lennon?" unintentionally sounding like an interrogator, a hopeful fan, or St. Peter. John, in the voice as familiar as a father's to millions of us, croaked, "Yeah." He had lost 80 percent of his blood volume and died of hypovolemic shock by the time they reached Roosevelt Hospital. I thought of how Paul McCartney said that one of the last times he saw him, John hugged him and said quietly, "Touching is good."

"Will we ever see John again?" Starbuck asked. He was near tears.

I paused, because I wasn't sure of my voice. It seems impossible we can lose people along the way as if they were only eyeglasses or extra sets of keys. I told Starbuck that through John's music and films we can be with him and the Beatles anytime we want, and that books and paintings and films and music and theater are like wonderful friends because they contain the best that human beings have ever thought and felt.

I rubbed the back of my neck and looked over the top of my glasses at Starbuck in the rearview mirror. It was a sure tell of unease, but he was only four. Besides, I thought I meant it, that stuff about the miracle of art.

Yes, I do.

Coming to Know a Place

To say that beginning writers resist revision is a redundancy. If they understood its necessity they'd already be unbeginners. Writing teachers ease them into it by telling them to do a "Save As" with their documents, so they'll always have the original drafts to go home to. Nothing is lost, we say, and it'll be okay.

Older writers too sometimes abandon work at the very moment that frustration with not-knowing might have led to a breakthrough. We toss aside drafts in a heat-panic, like throwing off blankets in the middle of the night—get off me! we cry.

None of us know the scope of the task when we start. But getting to know the sentences' landscape and people is necessary, and all we can do is stick with it. In reality, there's no going back.

〜〜

Crazy Larry called from Chicago to say he'd been trying to imagine my new life in Louisiana. His mental draft was pretty vague—that rural area down there, he said, field hands and old cars like you'd see in Havana—and I let it go on for a while because he was amusing. When I finally told him he was completely wrong, he demanded a truth, if his wasn't it.

Certain facts come easy, such as the population of Lake Charles (71,000) and the greater metropolitan area (200,000). There's a small state uni and a community college, a decent library system, several small museums, any number of good restaurants, and a river that flows down through three lakes to the Gulf of Mexico, thirty miles away. It's Acadiana.

But my impressions are still like coddled eggs, unset and easily broken. Our priorities have been to care for the family, get moved in, and learn new jobs, so we don't know much about the region, haven't taken long drives or even been to any festivals, though Lake Charles is called the Festival Capital of Louisiana. I never know the places that students name when I ask where they're from. The pharmacist, letting a long line of customers build behind me, insists on explaining—twice—how to get to the road headed south out of Baton Rouge—he begins to draw a map—that has all the former plantations—the phone rings and the drive-through buzzes but he carries on—and insists we stop at the one French bakery—the cream puffs are good, but oh lord he could just eat that bread for dessert—that outranks all the rest.

〜〜〜

The real name of the city we left behind, Champaign, is a geographical term for open, level country; prairie cut with streams. A little to my dismay, it's champaign here too, but its use is more diversified: rice, hay, and sorghum are grown; innumerable bayous (streams) support fish hatcheries as well as shrimp, crawfish, and oyster aquaculture; above all, one notes the horses and cattle standing in pastures that start at the city limits and stretch to the Gulf, where oil rigs like tiny Monopoly houses dot the horizon.

In an attempt to better understand, we attended the Southwest District Livestock Show and Rodeo, now in its seventy-fourth year. The event produces scholarships, they say, and the university mascot is after all a cowboy on a bucking bronco. The domed coliseum where it's held is "under the operation of" the university and hosts campus sporting events, but the money for its construction was raised by a self-imposed parish (county) tax. It seems the dome, with its adjacent livestock pavilion and agricultural arena, gets far more use by ranchers and farmers in the region.

A minivan is unusual enough here to draw comments from strangers, and ours would be easy to find later among the pickups. There was pleasure in walking across the dirt and grass parking lot, not some hot-baked concrete plain, in being slowed to the pace of man and beast, and in antici-pating a long afternoon with nowhere else to be.

A gigantic trailer silkscreened with action shots of pro rodeo action sat at the entry gate. Its back door was being used as a porch by a dozen cow-boys on folding chairs, hats pulled low, drinking coffee and talking shop. The stock pavilion just beyond it was the size of a Walmart, divided into pens by horizontal steel bars bigger than my arms. Most of the animals had already been moved, but we strolled through looking at new calves, a few pigs (their sharp sour smell the only unpleasant one), and one dewlapped zebu with patient eyes that liked having its head scratched by curious chil-dren and me.

A middle-aged woman in boots handed a small brochure to me, to my wife, and to each of my sons. The boys expressed hopes it contained cou-pons for free food, but it was titled, "Your Entry Fees Are Paid." The cover showed a cowboy digging in his pocket for money, and a ghostly arm com-ing down—Middle Eastern robes blending with the curtains—to proffer a handful of dollar bills to the cashier. Inside it was filled with loads of tiny type that began:

"Almost any 'rodeo cowboy' can relate to talk about entry fees because, [sic] entry fees are one of his greatest expenses. Having someone pay all your entry fees would be any cowboy's dream.

"The good news of the Christian Gospel is simply that someone has paid in full everyone's entry fee for the National Finals up in the sky. The pay-ment was made by Jesus Christ, who died on a cross nearly two thousand years ago."

The boys and I climbed the bars of a tall gate to watch a cowboy shoo a dozen big horses from one pen into another. There was the thrill and shock of animals that big moving so quickly, their large intelligent eyes looking at us, the dust and movement a violence of beauty. We watched so long that the Baptist lady came by with her brochures, didn't recognize us, and pressed them on us again.

Our seats were halfway up the dome. Down on the coliseum floor someone was driving a sponsor's extended-cab pickup under a spotlight while the announcer narrated its qualities. Afterward a tractor dragged around a chain harrow to erase tracks pressed into the otherwise immaculate, pulverized dirt. Country and rock music blared on the coliseum's loudspeakers.

Just as the rodeo was about to start, Starbuck suddenly objected. "This is immoral," he said, reopening old discussions on the treatment of animals, including one, years ago, after we'd left a circus and found it picketed by PETA.

I wasn't sure this time how much he believed and how much he was nearly eleven, so while I was proud of him for taking a stance, I parried his every blow: We paid twelve dollars each for these tickets, and you didn't object then . . . we had hamburgers for lunch yesterday and are likely to have chili tonight . . . we haven't gotten out much since we moved here . . . it's a nice day, I'm out now, and I'm going to stay out . . . unless you have an extra minivan and can drive yourself home you're out for the day too . . . gimme a break and be quiet, boy. In the end, popcorn, nachos, cotton candy, and soda did wonders—a little depressing for what it said about the frailty of ethics, but the nachos were really, really good.

The show began with fifteen minutes of jumbotron videos depicting military service, with talk by an emcee on a horse about defending the American way. Near the end of it he said: "They took it out of our schools and they took it out of our government, but we're proud to say that *prayer* hasn't been taken out of the *rodeo!*" He led the coliseum in a long prayer and then the Pledge of Allegiance, and there was a laser show, indoor fireworks, and more loud music on vaguely patriotic themes (including Springsteen's "Born in the USA," a common irony).

While hundreds of kids in the audience waved parti-colored light sabers and glow necklaces, a phalanx of tweens advanced on the floor and stood in the heavy smoke from the fireworks. They were stoic as Marines, never once squinted or made faces or waved their hands in front of their mouths and noses. Here, the emcee intoned, was the future of America; kids raised in this respectful environment "will become farmers, research scientists . . . soldiers who will serve as so many have. But above all, they'll become *the greatest thing that's ever existed*! American!" The coliseum air pressurized with cheers.

Then the rodeo proper began, an intricate and complete entertainment. There were the events you might expect: roping and bronc riding and barrel racing and bull riding and a halftime show where kids tried to rope and drag calves three times their weight into a square marked in the middle of the floor. Not a second was wasted: there were the competitions themselves, measured in tenths of seconds; commentary on the performances; instant replays on the big screens; banter between the mounted emcee and a rodeo clown; more indoor fireworks; reminders to buy from the coliseum vendors; giveaway contests for those who shouted loudest; invitations to reconsider the Dodge Ram shining under the lights; reminders to patronize local businesses; special appearances on the mezzanine by the hosts of a local Fox affiliate, multiplied by the jumbotrons; and loud music filling any gap.

The clown, whose name was Liesl, of all things, was pure vaudevillian corn, his routine a mix of *Hee Haw* and something more ancient, like Punch and Judy. Under the makeup and floppy clothing he was at least middle-aged and probably well beyond, no longer faking tiredness and sore feet. Workers placed a high-tech clown barrel, all steel and corporate logos, in the middle of the coliseum floor for his safety, and my boys and I held out hopes a bull would go for him before it was over. But it was two young cowboys who distracted the bulls so their riders could escape after the buzzer, while Liesl cracked bad jokes at a safe distance and three hard-looking riders with lariats stood guard behind him like mounted police or cavalry.

In the breaks Liesl told groaners and stretchers that made him out to be crafty-stupid, whiny, and lazy. He also worked a little blue, with stories about how the wife of his friend who had nine kids shouldn't be bending over to pick up laundry anymore. All this gave the straight-man emcee on his spangled horse many opportunities to disapprove. The emcee's voice, booming from his wireless mike, was part Rush Limbaugh and part Don Pardo.

"Liesl!" he cried in astonishment and disapproval at every fifth line. (Say it aloud now, starting as high and ending as low as you can, with the extreme disappointment you'd express if your kid turned down her full ride to Sarah Lawrence.)

None of this is to suggest falsehood. It would be typically academic to suggest the rodeo as a sport is mere simulacrum of work performed by man and horse in the job of ranching. But there's nothing artificial about some one-ton beast trying to snap your spine. After the first bronc rider in the program was thrown, the sports medicine people from the university came out, and he was taken to the hospital for x-rays.

The rodeo *felt* authentic, if authenticity is in question, neither concocted for the tourist trade nor of a second-order kitsch like pro wrestling, family truck stops, or the expressions of porn actors. It was entertainment in one of the oldest senses: "To keep up, maintain, to keep (someone) in a certain frame of mind," an expression and reinforcement of regional community. It's what corporatized, reality-show America pines for, and it's why so many women have a weakness for cowboys instead of for midlevel managers, provosts, or bloggers.

〜〜〜

I can tell you about Sale Road and Ryan Street, down which I commute among expensive three-quarter-ton pickups with crew cabs and duals. I know the part of campus where I do business, the supermarket where I'm told the rich people shop, and across the street, the mini-storage compound with our stuff in it. A quarter mile further on there's a bakery with delicious doughnuts, king cakes, and triple-sized after-school snow cones.

I'm also getting a feel for the new house. Not the exterior yet, with its little Asian-inspired gardens inside brick screening walls set with wrought gates, all of which Wolfie says will be useful in the zombie apocalypse. Most of my time is spent inside, so I'm starting to know the noises the house makes, and how the light shifts around through the day. Geckoes gather after dusk on the outside of windowpanes to eat bugs attracted by our lights. They present their most vulnerable side, pale bellies and delicate toe pads, and in return our indoor cats jump at them in vain and drag stuff—tomatoes, sink strainers, brushes, grocery receipts, books—off sills and counters as they fall madly back.

A few of the lizards, having stared through the windows for so long, decide to run in on the hinged side of doors when they open. Some of them pause, fatally hesitant to commit to one life or the other, and are crushed flat between jamb and door when it closes. They dry there, colors preserved and shapes surprisingly intact, like pressed flowers. You'd need a paint scraper to get them off now, since the former owner obviously never bothered, and a couple dollars in postage to mail them to Crazy Larry, with a nice note saying enjoy some Louisiana jerky.

My sons, horrified at first by the evidence of these accidents, have a sound now to accompany the sight of them stuck to the wood: HUNH!, they shout, stretching themselves rigid and bug-eyed—presumably the last thing a lizard does when surprised at finding itself in a new place with unknown forces closing in.

⌇⌇

Crazy Larry said it was seven degrees in Chicago and didn't believe giant bugs were beating themselves to death against my windows. In fact, I said, termite swarms had also descended, their discarded wings like falling snow in the headlights. I told him about the geckoes, and he asked if there was anything at all that could be done to stop them. I said stray cats ate the geckoes and other lizards.

"Oh, so you have a cat problem," he said.

No, I said. Stray dogs and gators eat the cats, and locals in pickup trucks run down dogs and gators for sport. Many of those people smoke, drink, and love fried foods. Thus is the fragile balance of life maintained.

He was concerned.

I assured him I'd get the book done, but the system I'd worked for years to get into, in order to have a writing life, required I do *everything* and *do it all well*. My time to finish the book, if I could hold off panic now, would come at the end of other tasks.

"Sounds to me like you got yourself in the wrong system," he said.

The system would purify itself, I said, giving me more time and resources to write the longer I was in it. I said it was like the *Apollo* spacecraft: you shed stages as you went, the goal being to reach a simple, elegant version of self, radiant as the moon. I didn't know if that was true, but Larry enjoys metaphors.

"Well, listen," he said, "all it really takes is food and water, right? What else do you have to do?"

I started deducting hours, days, weeks for obligations other than writing.

Larry said, "My employees thought they were too busy. I said we'd get temps or student workers in to help. Then they wanted to argue they'd have to train the temps and didn't have time for that either. I said they'd invest ten hours in training and get thirty hours freed-up. In a forty-hour week, that's a 75 percent return on a 25 percent investment of time.

"Let's look at *your* portfolio," he said.

I detailed the rest of my semester.

"Get rid of that," he said. "All of it. No reading, no grading. Cancel all your classes. Teaching at a university is not writing the book. Let somebody else drive visitors around. Postpone the dentist. Don't cook; eat cold cuts. Your kids can do without two weeks of Daddy playing with them."

I said I knew some of those guys. And I noted he didn't suggest I ignore his calls. I supposed I could get a sitter sometimes. Childcare was expensive.

"There's a price to be paid to get to Shangri-La," he said.

I told him that in the fall an unforeseen deadline had loomed, and I was asked to choose a topic for a spring lit seminar before the administrator's cigarette could burn down to the filter. Poverty, I'd blurted, regretting it even as the word passed my lips like acrid smoke. Now it was proving a hard sell. I'd put *The Grapes of Wrath* on the reading list so I could revisit a book I'd read and appreciated at eighteen. Back then I was half a semester from dropping out of community college and another few months from enlisting, but there were so many things I didn't know then that I didn't even know that. Steinbeck had resonated with me, but some of my students were resisting the novel.

"Do you remember that scene where the Joads are leaving their farm for good?" I said. "They get excited to get on the road to California, the promised land, so they start throwing things on the truck in the middle of the night. The men slaughter the last couple of pigs, which can't be brought alive. Ma packs the meat in salt kegs, and, 'as Noah cleaned the ribs, and the spines and leg bones of all the meat he could, she put them in the oven to roast for gnawing purposes.'

"'Be nice to have pork bones for breakfas',' she says."

"Those are hard people," I said. "Bones for breakfast. Talk about doing what you have to do. Of course there's no Shangri-La waiting at the end of *their* voyage, but they can't know that."

Crazy Larry said he and I would do whatever was necessary to get to the promised land of our ambitions. Everyone else would stop to tan their hides and scrape rust off their pots. A sandstorm would be coming and they'd want to refold laundry for the trip. He and I would cut off our saddlebags and leave wives and children behind, since they might not be fast enough to make it to the walls. Somebody had to survive to tell their tales in order to honor them. He laughed a little hysterically.

"So you're saying we'll end up eating our horses and then roasting their bones," I said.

"That's right. And years from now we'll *still* be running, on foot, across the salt flats with your grown sons in pursuit, the same way you tracked and ran down *your* father. And they'll be these *giant* men, feet dragging off shaggy ponies, bellowing 'Daddy' into the wind and hoping to hurt us real bad if only they can catch us. 'Da-*ddy*! Ya shoulda played with us more, Daddy-*Paddy*! Hear us, old man? We're coming for ya, and yer buddy Crazy Larry, too!'"

I was laughing now too. "And everybody who visits Shangri-La will be jealous of the stories about us eating our horses, and they'll wish they'd eaten their horses too."

∼∼∼

When I compare Lake Charles to other places I've known—let's say, Schaumburg, Illinois, which is not too far from Larry's house—there's not the same infrastructure or material culture, so it obviously feels much different. In Schaumburg, which is formed like an amoeba around the nucleus of its mega-mall—"Get the 411 . . . Woodfield has the finest collection of department stores and specialty shops in the Great Lakes region"—all that money has been poured into a tidal wave of concrete and consumerism. It's made and remade, but one must have money to participate, and then only in specific, rigid roles.

Here, things feel more open. There's an old-fashioned downtown and boardwalk (renovated with hurricane money), a mall, strip malls all over town, scattered big-box stores, bars, churches, parks, hospitals, stadium, but no central point where everyone is channeled for gain. (Not the university, as it was in Champaign, and not even the casinos, which are surprisingly marginalized.) There are a few tall buildings but lots of greenery too, and nowhere the blinding glare of pavement to the horizon. There are hummingbirds in the bottlebrush trees in my circle drive, white herons on my lawn, a national wildlife refuge south of town.

"Biomass," the poet's friend said with a sneer, his sum for all of southern Louisiana.

〜〜

Howard Nemerov, in "The Swaying Form: A Problem in Poetry": "The poet, if he has not attained to a belief in the existence of God, has at any rate got so far as to believe in the existence of the world; and . . . this, sadly but truly, puts him, in the art of believing, well out in front of many of his fellow-citizens, who sometimes look as if they believed the existence of the world to be pretty well encompassed in the sensations they experience when they read a copy of *Time*."

〜〜

That may be my first true impression of Louisiana: It *exists*. I thought so from the first visit to Lake Charles, when, driving around, I felt a palpable gravity in each neighborhood or area I encountered. A pleasant, wide street of scattered old homes, many of them converted to businesses such as barbershops, gives way in a single turn to an overgrown road along the tracks, a rusty caboose converted to a takeout seafood shack, its handwritten sign out front advertising fried gar.

City streets quickly become elevated paved roads between deep ditches that drain into bayous running through the city. There are no shoulders or guardrails on most of these roads; I imagine that in this open society texters are given the freedom to run off into ditches, break their heads in the crash, drown, then get eaten by beasties.

People own tools and do the work themselves. There are no wild animal trapping businesses to remove raccoons from your attic, since everybody owns guns and traps or knows someone who does. Folks meander through their yards, gather under a spreading live oak at a barbecue stand at lunch hour. Some joke but more state calmly that they don't believe they'll live long, so they plan to enjoy themselves. It's slower, apparently, this life, but what's that mean? Fatalism? Less ambition? Settledness and satisfaction?

As a newcomer, you eat the tail and suck the head, and then what?

The roller rink sells frozen pickle juice in little cups for a quarter. The kids lick them like popsicles.

So now you know, but what is it you know?

Before lunch (Cajun sausage and peach cobbler) in the university cafeteria, Dr. Blevins gets all sly and sexy, says he knows how glad my family and I are to be here with him and our colleagues in this place at this time, and I'm convinced he's right.

~~~

The young veteran of our wars, a former Scout and intelligence-gatherer, is tattooed and Brylcreemed, but then he is from Texas. He's also begun to publish in foreign policy and military affairs journals, using papers he's been writing for rhetoric classes as a returning undergrad.

I bought him lunch, and he suggested we take our families on a picnic sometime soon. I asked if he had a place in mind, and he mentioned a mock Iraqi village where our troops play war games to prepare them for the real thing. The village, he said, is out in the middle of nowhere and has secret rooms and a tunnel that goes from a basement into the trunk of a bombed-out car. The kids would love it. He's still in the Guard and knows the place well. American OPFOR soldiers and civilians, hired for their ethnicity and language, inhabit the village, wearing traditional Middle Eastern garb made in China, but there'd be a lull between training cycles soon, it would be dead, and we should go then.

It's often pointed out that the United States runs its current wars with little attention to them at home, beyond political flourishes about supporting the troops. A twinge of—what was it?—*apprehension* gave me pause, the weird coincidence of that other world put down here, of all places, an hour away, and me still trying to get my bearings. Also: I know how impromptu adventures with army buddies often go, which is why I've steered clear of them for the last decade while my children were small. I had a book to finish. Still.

My boys and I left the house at three in the afternoon to get to Matt's house by four, but we had to stop for chips, salsa, and drinks, and I nearly got us lost in the rain. Matt, his wife, their infant twins, and his sister-in-law were already in an SUV when we got there, signaling their belief in the army motto "On Time, on Target." We'd convoy a short distance to the mock village—he said it was twenty minutes from the house—have some chicken wraps and almond cookies, the kids would run around, and we'd get home before my wife got off work at eight.

It took half an hour driving through piney woods just to reach Fort Polk. We didn't go in the main gate, and the narrow road was deserted. I've never been on a military installation so open and unguarded. Ranges appeared in clearings on both sides, and frequent signs warned of unexploded munitions, but there were no fences or cameras I could see, and I don't know what would keep civilians from trying to harvest brass for scrap or any unspent ordinance for more nefarious purposes.

I know vets who enjoy being around the active military, but I'm sensitive to the mass of that whole galaxy of discipline, containment, and order. Deep down I'm nervous that if get too close I might be pulled back in, or that I'll have forgotten some rule and get yelled at—by armed federal troops. When Frenchy and I stayed the night, for economy's sake, on navy bases during a recent research trip, the base loudspeakers played "Colors," and I had no memory of what to do. Stop the car? Get out of the car? Civilian hand on chest? Which way to face? The twinned neuroses of inclusion and exclusion.

Troops in uniform sprawled lifelessly on bleachers at one passing range, but otherwise there was no one but us as we crisscrossed the military reservation and Kisatchie National Forest for the next hour and a half. Blackened trees from controlled burns pressed in on the road there was a glimpse of an old graveyard, a crossroads with two ramshackle houses and a mobile home. A sign—Schoolbus Exit—was nailed to a tree in the forest, which made my boys laugh enough to briefly forget their imminent mutiny. I stayed well back so the SUV wouldn't kick up a rock and break my windshield, and thought of my minivan's street tires, muffler, tie rods, struts. Good dog.

Sometime later we rounded the hundredth curve, hopped a rise, sank into the dip, and found a waterfall pouring off a hill to the left, its torrent flowing deeply across the road and spreading into the trees. I hit the brakes, but Matt accelerated and hit the flood with an enormous spray and splash. His tires hydroplaned then sank, back axle and differential disappearing in the water. I thought surely his truck would stall or even be swept off the concrete apron into the bog downstream, and in a flash I saw his babies strapped into their car seats. But the SUV powered through and then was sitting high and dry on the gravel road on the other side.

"Are we going through that?" Starbuck asked.

"Through what?" Wolfie wanted to know and looked up from his iPod.

I got out and stood watching the water. There were no tow services, cell coverage, or other people for miles. Backing up took time, and we were losing light. It poured again, briefly, with tropical intensity.

On the blacktop Matt finally noticed his flat tire and pulled over but had no tools, embodying the army motto *Volens et potens* (Willing and able), but not *Semper preparate*. I helped lower the spare from under the truck, but my wrench didn't fit his security lugs. I suggested we eat there on the side of the road and go get help, but Matt was intent on the picnic in Iraq.

While we discussed it, a pickup stopped. The two guys who got out looked a little rough but couldn't have been nicer. They said they saw we had little ones, that it's easy to get a flat out here since there's spent M-16 cartridges everywhere that'll puncture a tire in a heartbeat, and that Matt's spare looked mostly flat too.

"You ain't goin' *nowhere*," the younger of the two said.

I don't mean to be ungrateful, but a chivalrous code can be a veneer for less chivalrous behaviors—not everyone is entitled to protection—and there are codes within codes. Because they offered to help, for instance, we weren't allowed to use their wrench to do the work; the younger guy insisted on taking the filthy tire off himself and putting on the spare, even if one didn't care for how he tightened the nuts without using a star pattern to get the torque even. Matt was a little cool to them, and after they left he explained that the nearby hamlet is a well-known sundown town, and that when he trains guardsmen here, men and women of color are advised to stay in the van or else not get separated from their comrades. Supporting the troops has its limits.

We'd have to come back for the suv if we were to complete our picnic mission, and now we had four adults and four kids in my van, and the chicken wraps were getting cold. Matt knelt on the floor and pointed the way: off the blacktop road, across that set of train tracks and that gravel road, onto something that looked like a dirt parking lot, then forward through a hummocked plain, stretching for miles, that served as a drop zone and was dotted with hull-down firing positions for armored vehicles. The sun was setting on the prairie, and an advance guard of wild turkeys ran down the middle of the dirt track in front of the van. Like the infantryman he is, Matt had his military topo map folded to the area we needed, sealed with green duct tape in a Ziploc, the relevant route marked in red grease pencil on the plastic.

"Turn left up here," he said.

"Here?" I asked.

"Sure, why not," he said.

We reached Tofani, the interchangeably Iraqi/Afghani village, about two and a half hours later than planned. It's a U.S. Army Joint Readiness Training area but was deserted, as Matt said it would be. We drove in under an arched gate, past the combat outpost (a drab walled compound for U.S. forces—think the Baghdad green zone on a tiny scale), and the village was ahead on a wide gritty street. The buildings were all earthen-colored; inside we saw they'd been knocked together with conex containers, 2×4s, and plywood. Sure enough, a back panel in a file cabinet in the "Internet Club" opened to a secret "bad-guy" infirmary.

One of the objectives for training here was to "turn" the village. Good decisions (offering food, water, and medical supplies; interacting appropriately with the locals) led to tips on where insurgents are hiding, which led to opportunities for combat raids. Poor decisions (miscommunication and disrespect) had bad outcomes, such as mock death. All was watched and judged by octs (observer, coach, trainers), who "observe unit performance, control engagements and operations, teach doctrine, coach to improve unit performance, monitor safety and conduct professional after action reviews (AARS)."

The place was creepy as hell, completely surreal, last outpost of the zombie apocalypse, and we happily had our picnic under a metal shed while it rained, again. Matt's wife and I were having a nice conversation about how she got her bachelor's degree online while he was still active duty—now she's a teacher—when their little boy fell through the picnic table and knocked his head against the bench seat on the way down. We were something like forty kilometers in the middle of piney woods, prairie, and bayous, but he was okay. My own boys loved the place and begged to keep the .223 and .50-caliber blank rounds they found everywhere on the ground and were disappointed when I wouldn't allow it. After supper we all strolled up Main Street, pointing out fake laundry hanging on a line, wrecked cars and buses, and blasted bicycles, and we did some window shopping in mock market stalls that displayed piles of beat-up pots and pans, filthy computer monitors, broken space heaters, and stacks of old TVs. In one of the buildings I found a defunct copier and file cabinets furry with rust that would have been a boon for the hard-strapped English Department, but I left them there.

Matt said there was another mock village nearby, the one with the secret tunnel my boys would most like to see, so we drove out the far side of Tofani. The next village should have been right there, but it wasn't, and was that bend in the road the place that marked the other thing? His babies were screaming from their car seats in the back of my van, his wife trapped between them. I caught a glimpse of her face in the rearview and did him a favor and called it. A lot of backtracking later, I dropped him at his SUV, and he limped along in it and got air in the reputed Klan town. I kept his family with me in case the tire wasn't sound, and when we were back at their house I thanked his wife and asked, out of curiosity, whose idea all this was. His, she said, with the aggravated forthrightness but good-natured acceptance of a military spouse.

My boys and I stopped at a Wendy's on the way home because it was late and we could. They had loved the whole unscripted adventure, now that the boredom and fear were over, and I was glad for them.

I had recently read Mary Ruefle's essay "On Fear," in which she brings up Kierkegaard's idea of "striv[ing] to become what one already is," that "education was the curriculum one had to run through in order to catch up with oneself." Sometimes it's as hard to reconcile the different parts of a life as it is to reconcile beautiful and ugly, and this was one more chance to study on mine.

~~~

I get the leashes to take the dogs out. The boys are half-asleep on kitchen stools, eating oatmeal. Countess Tolstoy, a cross between a Highland cow and a water buffalo, bounces merrily, a come-hither look over her shoulder, nails clawing helplessly at the tile floor. But once outside she doesn't want to get her feet wet in the heavy dew, and I have to pull her onto the lawn, where she microsniffs every blade of grass suspiciously. I wonder how she reads this landscape. It's still dark, but the moon is up. An owl hoots. Neighbors' houses are darker cutouts against the sky, and clouds from the Gulf cross over low and fast. I go get the other dog.

The boys get dressed, pack their backpacks, and join me outside. This is the first place they've had to ride a bus to school. I wonder if I'll embarrass them in my pajama shorts, Crocs, and T-shirt; instead they ask for extra kisses to put in their pockets for later. The bus turns off the main road, strobes firing and turn signals blinking, roars over the culvert and squeals to a stop in a cloud of diesel stink at the end of our driveway.

I'm left holding the leash of Count Tolstoy and wave at the bus's darkened windows. The boys have told me I'm to stand there until the bus winds its way through the neighborhood and comes around again on the main road, going the other way, so the dog and I stand there in the quiet, being bitten by large black mosquitoes. Sometimes late at night a parish mosquito truck passes by with its fogger hissing, and the sound takes me back to being a kid. There was a taste to that spray. I haven't talked to Eric or anybody else in my hometown in a while. There's a lot of people I haven't talked to lately. It's getting light now.

Then the bus emerges down the way, gains speed quickly and roars past with its tires humming. I wave, the driver honks once, and my sons are gone a second time. It's the same every morning, except sometimes, to their great amusement, the dog is squatting as the bus comes back by, and I'm smiling hugely like a big dummy, waving my plastic-baggie glove like it's all a good time and more to come. The poop is hot and well-formed in the cold wet grass.

~~~

In the geography of the sentence, all you can really do is work at it, time and again, in hopes of making whatever is well sung.